LETTERS to
Exodus
CHRISTIANS

LETTERS 1 to Exodus CHRISTIANS

comfort and hope for those
who have trouble going to church

Edward Hays

Marillac Center
4200 South 4th Street
Leavenworth, KS 66048

Forest of Peace Notre Dame, IN

Founded in 1865, Ave Maria Press is a ministry of the Indiana Province of Holy Cross.

www.forestofpeace.com

ISBN-10 0-939516-82-9   ISBN-13 978-0-939516-82-7

Cover photo by Steve Woods, courtesy of www.sxc.hu.

Cover and text design by Andy Wagoner.

Printed and bound in the United States of America.

This book is dedicated to all

Roman, Episcopal, Lutheran, Methodist,
and Presbyterian Catholics,
as well as other Christians who,
while not attending church,
continue striving to live their faith.

contents

preface

Why I Wrote This Book

As a seventy-seven-year-old retired Roman Catholic priest and former pastor, I felt pushed by the Spirit to write this book. Having been ordained for fifty years, my heart aches for those once called the "fallen away," who no longer attend church on a regular basis or do not attend at all. While I write primarily for those of my own religious tradition, this book is applicable to Exodus Christians of all other churches as well since we share a common creed and faith.

In the past forty years, the majority of North American churches have experienced an "exodus" (or great departing) of many members. Currently, an estimated 70 percent or more of Roman Catholics no longer attend church on a regular basis, yet they continue to think of and publicly identify themselves as Catholic. Estimates for non-attendance in the other Catholic, non-Roman churches are about the same or even greater. Some studies show the figure for weekly attendance at a religious service in the United States to be about 45 percent. This percentage is more than twice as high as other developed Western countries, where the average is about 15 to 21 percent, and in Britain, where it is only 7 percent. However, the unusually high American average for attendance at weekly religious services is suspect since it is widely acknowledged that people often exaggerate when they are surveyed about their daily prayer and weekly worship habits.

The numbers of those joining this New Exodus of people no longer going to church regularly increases daily, and will likely continue to do so with each new generation. For me, these Exodus Christians are not simply percentage numbers or faceless people. They are good friends of mine, former students, converts, family members, and past parishioners. They are commonly termed "fallen away" from the faith. But many of them didn't *fall* away; they were *pushed away*. These include those who were divorced and entered a second marriage without undergoing the long and often difficult process of canonical annulment. Others were pushed away because their gay or lesbian sexual orientation is defined by the church as a disorder, along with any natural expression of their sexuality being declared sinfully unnatural. The departure of still others is because the Church of Rome persists with its antiquated sexual exclusivity that denies women equal status with men in the ministry of the church. Most recently, many have left because of the ongoing exposure of sexual abuse scandals and the accompanying failure of leadership that have rocked the Roman Catholic Church since 2001.

The causes of this New Exodus are many and varied and sometimes traumatic. But perhaps the most common and widespread reason for people leaving their churches is paralleled by this real-life story. A good friend of mine is a retired professor and a grandfather. He told me that one day his granddaughter announced to him that, after being married for seven years, she was divorcing her husband, Jack. My friend was shocked since he had always felt that his granddaughter had a good marriage. So he asked her, "Does Jack abuse you in any way, physically or verbally?" She silently shook her head no. "Does Jack drink or use drugs?" She replied, "No." "Well then, is he a dependable

husband, does he go to work and support you and your two
children?" She nodded her head and said, "Yes, Jack's a very
hard-working man and a caring father." My friend then asked
gently, "Is Jack having an affair with another woman?" "No,"
she replied, "I'm sure that he loves only me." Confused, my
friend was left with only one logical question, "Why then are
you divorcing him?" His granddaughter's eyes filled with sadness as she said, "Because Jack's boring!"

I propose that the vast majority of those who have stopped
going to church regularly have not done so because they are
lax or indifferent, but simply because they've been bored out
of it! They have been bored away, finding worship uninspiring
and, most of all, empty of nourishment. Any building that titles
itself a "church" carries an implicit assurance that it is a place
of spiritual nourishment and inspiration. The majority of those
who no longer attend church, except for funerals, weddings,
and perhaps Christmas or Easter, are those who have returned
home from going to church again and again still hungry. These
hungry, un-churched people are too often met with condemna-
tion instead of being treated with understanding compassion.

This majority within the church mirrors the vast multitude
for whom Jesus felt great pity in the Gospel of Mark. That evan-
gelist relates how Jesus and his disciples, seeking to escape the
crush of the crowd, went off to a deserted place to rest, only to
be followed there by a multitude of thousands. The gospel relates how when Jesus saw "the vast crowd, his heart was moved
to pity for them, for they were like sheep without a shepherd;
and he began to teach them many things" (Mk 6:34). Each of
the four gospels contains a story of this event, yet the authors
do not tell us what it was that Jesus taught the crowds, but only
that what drew them into the wilderness was a desire to hear

his teachings. The shepherd of Galilee taught them and then attended to their physical hunger by feeding them in that deserted place, just as Moses had done for the people of the first Exodus.

This image of Jesus teaching and feeding the multitude who were like sheep without a shepherd holds the incentive and purpose for my writing this book, for surely Jesus spoke to the real hunger of those weary thousands who longed to hear words of hope and compassion. We are told their hunger was satisfied, and it is my fervent hope that this book will likewise feed many who today wander hungry, without a shepherd or a sheltering sheepfold.

The New Exodus

The story of the great Exodus told in the Bible relates how Moses led the Hebrews out of their enslavement in Egypt into the desert, leading them in the end to the land God had promised them. The term "Exodus" doesn't just refer to their departure from Egypt, but includes their forty long years of wandering in the desert before reaching the Promised Land. The term "New Exodus" is appropriate today for those Christians who are departing—or have already departed from—attending church on a regular basis or at all, and the subsequent spiritual and religious wandering that most of them continue to do.

Some scholars believe the multitude Moses led out of Egypt was not made up of a single people, the Hebrews, but was rather a ragged collection of oppressed peoples of various origins suffering as slaves at the heavy hands of the Egyptians. But by their shared communal departure and wandering in the dessert, they were forged together into a single people known as the Hebrews, or Israelites. Perhaps by design of the Spirit—the same Spirit who inspired that first Exodus—those who today make up the New Christian Exodus will be forged together into a common body. The Bible tells us that the Exodus from Egypt was both willed and inspired by God, and not merely some political insurrection by oppressed classes seeking independence. Is it not possible that sacred history will record today's ongoing Christian Exodus also as a work of the Spirit—both willed and inspired by God, who continues to make all things new?

Why Letters?

"Epistle" comes from the Greek for any written communication, and there are twenty-one such communications or letters in the New Testament. They were sent by early apostolic missionaries, such as Paul of Tarsus, to encourage and strengthen the small, original Christian communities in the ancient world, such as Greece and Rome. I use this same literary genre in this book for the same purposes of encouraging and strengthening (if not stretching) the faith of those who do not attend worship services in church on a regular basis, or at all. Some of these are actual letters that I have written and have slightly edited to preserve the privacy of the receivers. Others flow from lunch conversations or from exchanges in spiritual direction that I have formatted into the style of a letter.

It is my deepest hope that you find these new epistles of encouragement and instruction as helpful as if they had been written directly to you, the reader. I pray that the same Spirit who guided the writers of the New Testament epistles will inspire all of us who are experiencing the New Exodus of Christians from many churches and walks of life. May the Spirit lead us, whether we journey within the ranks of the great departure or walk alongside the multitude, trying to comfort, strengthen, and share a little hope.

ONE

Letters to
Individual Exodus
Christians

Letter to My Brothers and Sisters
of the Exodus

Dear Ralph and Susan,

The clergy and many other members of the Church refer to you as "lax Catholics" or "ex-Catholics," terms that even perhaps you yourselves use to identify your religious affiliation. "Non-practicing," along with the derogatory "fallen away" (as in fallen outside of the Church by sin), are common terms for those who fail to meet the litmus test of a faithful Catholic: attending Mass on all Sundays and holy days. But rejoice; you're not fallen away outside the Church! If you are an ex-Catholic, that "ex" can stand for "exodus." An Exodus Christian is one who has or is departing from the Church in the New Exodus. Know that you are one among the majority of American Catholic Christians who in ever-escalating numbers have stopped attending church on a regular weekly basis. While presently most of you do attend religious services on special occasions, such as funerals, weddings, baptisms, Christmas, and Easter, many of you will stop doing even this in the coming years.

The fact that a large and ever-growing majority of the faithful no longer believes weekly church attendance is a condition for being a good Christian is pastorally and theologically challenging. Part of the rich theology of the Church is the concept of the "sense of the faithful"; in Latin, *sensus fidelium*. This means that the ongoing experience of the majority of the faithful is an important source for theology and a basis for renewed interpretation of Church teachings. The law of the Church affirms this principle in Canon 27, where it says, "Custom is the best interpreter of laws."

The actual practice of the faithful over a period of time confirms or defines the meaning of the law. Returning then to the requirement for weekly attendance at worship, does the present lived experience of the majority of the believers challenge us as the community of the Church to reinterpret that requirement? Perhaps we ought no longer view this as a binding law for membership, but rather as the ideal and a spiritually wholesome religious activity.

The origin of Christian Sunday worship was the gathering of believers on the first day of the week for a religious meal, during which they recounted the teachings of Jesus and listened to letters written by apostles such as Paul. These weekly gatherings of small groups of believers were dynamic and life-giving because they were intimate and took place in private homes. For the first couple hundred years, as long as these home church communities remained small, they were as vibrantly nourishing as fresh bread. "Small," "intimately personal," and "vibrantly nourishing" are hardly the terms used today to describe the usual Sunday worship.

Over the next two millennia the experience of Sunday worship evolved into an often rote practice or custom, rather than an intense, intimate spiritual experience. As church buildings grew larger and larger to accommodate entire city populations, worship became more and more impersonal and devoid of inspiration. Religious superstitions and sometimes overly zealous devotions developed related to the relics of saints and holy places. Good people struggled to be as faithful as they could to the teachings of Jesus. Their faith in God and their religious practices sustained them in times of great suffering—dire poverty, exploitation by many of those in power, sickness, and death.

Today, as an Exodus Catholic, you continue to practice your faith by striving to live the Christian values of the Gospel, even through the most troubling times. If you are asked if you practice your faith, you can answer, "Yes." And, if you are asked to what church you belong, you can honestly respond, "I'm a Roman Catholic." A Roman understanding of law is strikingly differently than an Anglo-Saxon understanding of law, from which we in the United States derive our legal system. In Rome, a red light at an intersection operates more as a suggestion than an absolute requirement that one must stop. Roman citizens stop—or do not—depending upon circumstances at the intersection, such as if the cross-traffic is negotiable or if there are no other vehicles approaching. John Allen, an American reporter in Rome, says that this subjective view of interpreting law by Romans doesn't lead to chaos, but rather to the flow of life. Allen says that the people of Rome realize that we are not pure spirits, and so we must be practical regarding law, including Church laws. So when Romans are confronted with some absolute law, they usually seek a practical adjustment, saying *"facciamo cosi"* or "Let's do it like this."

So, perhaps what we have been taught as absolute requirements for belonging to the Church are a little more adjustable than we have might have believed. Perhaps faithful commitment to the Gospel (and so to the heart of the Church) requires you in good conscience to fast from going to church—at least for a time—until some new life springs forth either within you or within the Church itself.

I conclude this letter to you, my brother and sister Exodus Christians, with the hope that it has helped you to view yourselves in a new yet very ancient light that confirms you are faithful members of the Body of Christ and of the Pilgrim People of

God. I pray you will continue to keep, and even grow in, the faith as practicing Catholic Christians striving to live according to the high standards of a disciple of Jesus.

Letter to Frank and Mary, Who Feel Alienated from the Church

Dear Frank and Mary,

Thanks for your most thoughtful note after our delightful reunion at Saturday's lunch. It seems impossible that it has been more than forty years since I had the two of you in religion class. Our lunch was in every way truly an Emmaus Eucharist. Both of you shared your sadness at leaving the church that once richly nourished you, just as those two disciples on the road to Emmaus poured out their sense of profound loss and hopelessness at the death of Jesus.

I applaud that, after you have tried parish after parish, you continue your mutual search for the Divine Mystery by attending the United Christian Church, in which you have found your need for worship satisfied. Jesus said that in God's heaven there were many houses, not simply one, and he also promised that wherever two or three were gathered together in his name he would be there. Regardless of the name on the door of the church, I'm convinced we can feel the touch of his presence there. Even if your aged mother is silently worried about you not attending church, bless her for her silence about your conduct though she fears that you have fallen away from the faith.

As I said at our lunch, like countless others, you are not fallen away! You have not left the church; rather, you have simply graduated from it! Both of you were born into the church, baptized as infants, and educated in Catholic schools, including college. Sunday after Sunday you were taught in the School of Holiness how to pray and love God, ways to be instruments of justice and peace, and to care for the poor, and now you've graduated! You need no weekly admonitions on how to practice your faith, as you've now incorporated that faith as the path of your life. Your graduation from the institutional church, like every graduation, should be a joyous event, but it isn't. Unfortunately for the majority of Catholic Christians, their church graduation gowns are woven with dreary threads of sadness, regret, anger, and for some, guilt.

Instead of being congratulated on becoming a religious graduate, be prepared to be judged by family and others as delinquent truants who are playing hooky from the One and Only School of Holiness. If only the church could be like good parents who wisely give their children both roots and wings. Churches should graft onto their members the ancient roots of the faith—of ritual, prayer, and tradition. Then, when they are mature, churches should to joyfully give them wings and allow them to fly out on their own.

You spoke of how depressing you found the negativity of the sermons and the scolding reprimands of the new pastor at your parish. The rise of a rigid fundamentalism in all churches, including yours, has sadly created a religion perpetually critical of our contemporary world. Religion as an inflexible and infallible arbitrator of morals has cast a gloomy pall over the modern world, eclipsing the God of joy and delight. If the preaching of the church were prophetic instead of only moralistic, then sermons would deal with war, the immoral amount of money spent on military armaments, and other gross injustices to the poor, elderly, and the migrant. Sadly, sexual issues instead of social issues are too often the subjects of sermons.

Jesus prayed at his last supper that his disciples might inherit his joy, but too many of today's eucharistic remembrances of his Last Supper seem to be radically void of joy. The old adage, "Sad is mad upside down," may explain the absence of joy

Letter to Bob on How to Grow Spiritually Without Attending Church

My Dear Bob,

I appreciated your letter in which you spoke of your disenchantment with the Church. I can guess such a letter wasn't easy to write to a priest, even if a retired one! And in there you wrote to me inquiring how to continue growing spiritually without the weekly support of going to church.

You said you were no longer a practicing Catholic. How we envision ourselves shapes our thinking, so I propose you don't look upon yourself as "non-practicing" because you've stopped attending church on a weekly basis. While it is certainly important, attending Sunday worship was never included in Jesus' list of works expected of his disciples. He expected far more of them than a passive hour a week, and so more is also expected of us as baptized Christians. We are to be actively involved in ongoing works like feeding the poor, never returning injury for injury, forgiving seventy times seven, never judging others, etc.

If you desire an examination to see if you qualify as a practicing Catholic Christian, I propose you read chapters 5 to 7 in Matthew's Gospel. In these chapters Jesus teaches the duties of his disciples, some of which are calls to perfection, such as his words about marriage, war and violence, and never offering resistance to evil. After reviewing those rigorous requirements expected of his disciples, I assure you that you will find the yardstick of weekly church attendance to be by far the easiest.

From its apostolic beginnings, the gathering of the Christian community on the first day of week was to support, strengthen, and encourage one another to live as the teacher Jesus desired.

From these weekly friendship gatherings, after reflecting on the gospel (in the beginning, oral stories and remembrances) and being nourished by sharing Holy Communion and the company of the community, they were sent forth, energized to be dynamic disciples.

Apparently, the opposite of that vibrant experience happens in most churches today since a majority—presently more than 70 percent of believers like you—have stopped attending church on a weekly basis. One can wonder how many of those who continue to faithfully attend Sunday worship also find it sterile but continue to do so out of pious habit or simple guilt.

Being an Exodus Christian isn't easy because it challenges you to be creative in finding spiritual expression and nourishment outside of attending church. You may already be experiencing a void in your life since you were indoctrinated as a child to be a religiously ritual person. There is almost an inbred affinity for sacred rituals and living according to a sacred calendar with its cycles of Advent, Christmas, Lent, Easter feasts, and holy days. While intellectually you "know" that everything and everywhere is crammed full of the Spirit of God, and is therefore holy, daily activities don't seem religious since they lack the sensorial feel of the stained-glass sacred.

Part of the challenge of being an Exodus Catholic Christian is the constant work of striving to experience the holy hidden inside the humdrum and human. While the distance from your head to heart is only a few inches, it might as well be 10,000 miles when it comes to tasting, feeling, and sensing the sacred in that which is so common and human. To experience the divine in the ordinary requires faith in that presence and persistence in seeking it. Paradoxically, more faith is required to be an Exodus Christian than to be a traditional Christian believer since you must practice Braille belief: believing without seeing.

In another letter to follow I will write you about how to celebrate the gospel sacraments of ordinary human life that do not require an ordained clergy, sacred buildings, or ecclesial rituals. Meanwhile, I encourage you to recall the potent words of Jesus that we would encounter him, and therefore grace, in the sacraments of the gospels: feeding the poor, visiting the sick and the imprisoned, sharing the grief of those burying their dead, being compassionate to the poor and needy, and forgiving all who offend you. Blessings on you and your quest to find God in the midst of the common events and gospel challenges of your daily life.

Letter to Beverly, Whose Son Is a Gay Exodus Christian

Dear Beverly,

Thank you for your letter, and in this letter I will attempt to answer to your questions. You wrote to me of your worries about your son who is gay and has stopped going to church except on Christmas and Easter, when he goes with you. I can understand your anxiety and distress for his soul since he no longer desires or practices being a Catholic Christian, but what impressed me was that you aren't distressed that your son is gay. In your letter you spoke of your love for him and your pride in your son because he is always kind to others, helpful to neighbors, and volunteers for various projects for the poor and homeless in your city. You confessed in your letter that you couldn't imagine God not also loving your son since he is such a good person. Still, you feel that this belief must be heresy since it contradicts what you read in your church paper and hear from the pulpit about homosexuals.

Beverly, I applaud your excellent theology! First, God's love is always unconditional, and secondly, your son is still a Catholic Christian, even if he attends church only with you on Christmas or Easter. I also commend you for your fidelity in loving your son regardless of his sexual orientation, a condition over which he personally has no choice. As for you being a heretic, the word means *choice*, and you've chosen a belief based on love, even if it's contrary to the position of your pastor or your church. Don't doubt; trust your love since God is love!

You asked me what I thought about what your pastor was preaching when he said that only those who faithfully followed all—and he emphasized *all*—of the Church's teachings may

receive Holy Communion. You continued that he also said all
lax members needed to be weeded out of the parish, even if that
meant the parish would be much smaller, since then it would
be purer and more dynamic. Your pastor's words about "weed-
ing out" those impure or sinful because they didn't accept all
the Church's teachings reminded me of a parable of Jesus. He
told the delightful story of a hired hand who discovered weeds
growing among wheat and asked his master if he should pull
up the weeds. The master said not to do so lest in attempting to
remove the weeds he do damage to the wheat, but rather to let
them grow together side by side until the harvest.

He spoke his weed parable to the pious of his day who ob-
jected to the fact that he enjoyed being in the company of those
they judged to be impure and sinners since they didn't keep the
religious laws. Jesus never explained the meaning of his para-
bles, but preachers often say this one deals with the possibility
of conversion, and how with time the weeds will evolve into
good wheat. However, it seems that this parable challenged his
listeners to question if they were they were the weeds or the
wheat. It likely also called to mind his famous radical words
to the pious Pharisees and law-abiding scribes, warning that
sinful tax collectors and prostitutes would enter heaven before
they would.

From an experience in my own life, I propose a further possibility to that story. Some years past I was directing a worker to
cut down some weeds, when he turned and said to me, "Do you
mean those wildflowers?" He then proceeded to instruct me by
naming all the wildflowers that I had called weeds! It was one
of those awakening moments in life that changed the way I saw
so-called weeds, and it also gave me an insight into this parable
of Jesus. The question I ask then is this: "Are the weeds in the

parable truly noxious (notorious) weeds, or are they wildflowers?" And, secondly, "Will our eyes be opened at the time of the Great Harvest, when those persons we judged as weeds will be praised by the Harvest Master for being more beautiful than the wheat?" I prefer to see your gay son—and all the others whom the righteously religious and the Church judge as sinners with such disdain—as the wildflowers of the kingdom, which God finds more valuable and appealing than the wheat.

So, I encourage you and other parents of homosexual children not to worry, especially not to judge their moral state, and to continue to lavish your love and affirmation upon them. As a parent you are a living image, a sacrament of God's paternal loving care. Your son is experiencing the love of God in your loving of him. I hope this letter will be an encouragement for you and will help to resolve some of religious concerns. As for your pastor, pray for him that he may experience a conversion of his heart so that it may become as tender and compassionate as the Good Shepherd's. Sadly, it takes little or no time to prepare and preach sermons condemning sins of morality; they are easy. What requires skill and effort is to preach and teach people how to pray and follow the path to holiness. Pray for your pastor.

I conclude wishing God's blessings on you and your son. May the Holy Spirit of Diversity gift him with the grace to wholeheartedly embrace the reality that God created him in his mother's womb, a homosexual man, a good, kindhearted, and loving man. In our society, for him to be authentically faithful to that divine design will require your unfailing love of him and God's unfailing grace. May the tender, motherly Spirit of God continue to guide you both.

Letter to Patrick, Who Hungers
for God but Feels Suffocated in Church

Dear Pat,

I hope both you and your family are well, and thank you again for your telephone call. I too regret that face-to-face conversations are no longer possible because of the many miles that now separate us from one another. The obstacle of distance, however, may actually be a gift for more thoughtful communication. Within written correspondence are two gifts. The first is to have both space and time to reflect on what was expressed in a letter before responding. The second gift is to be able to think twice as we put our thoughts to paper and see them in print before us. If we consider our exchange of letters as paper conversations, perhaps they could begin with "As I was saying," and conclude with asking, "What do you think about this?"

So I am grateful for the days that have passed since our telephone conversation, as it allowed me time to reflect upon what you said. I am writing both to affirm and to add some thoughts to what I said on the telephone. You spoke of your personal and painful contradiction of being hungry for God but suffering a sense of suffocation whenever you are at Mass. You had been a reader at Mass and found joy in that role in the liturgy, but now even that ministry leaves you hollow and alienated. You asked me how one could feel drawn to God but be repelled by worship of God.

Recent neurological studies have shown that humans are mentally hard-wired with distinctive nerve pathways in our brains for religious or spiritual experiences. The famous existential philosopher and atheist Jean-Paul Sartre wrote about this primitive hunger for the Divine in 1947: "Everything within me calls out for God." Since prehistoric times, before the appearance of any religion, our ancestors felt that same hunger. Our religious ancestors fed their hunger for the holy by experiencing it directly in creation. Just as we have lost much of our primitive sense of smell over the millennia, so we have also lost our ancestors' keen sense of the presence of the sacred in trees, rocks, rivers, and animals.

Their powerful epiphanies, or experiences of the Divine, led ancient peoples to make certain trees, rock outcroppings, or rivers into holy shrines, natural tabernacles of the Living Presence. Their worship at these natural shrines of the Divine that saturate all of creation did not make them unholy, but rather children of faith whose earthen worship was the first step in sacred awakening. Their reverential adoration or acknowledgement of the Divine Presence abiding in nature should be reclaimed, not abandoned.

Sadly, we who claim to possess the fullness of faith after just a couple millennia of indoor worship often lack the spiritual sensibility to directly experience God in creation. The present ecological crisis threatening the Earth and the greedy wholesale exploitation of natural resources only testify to our modern unbelief. To wantonly deface a church, synagogue, or mosque is a grievous sacrilege, but so is spray-painting graffiti on a canyon wall, dumping garbage along the roadside, or pouring toxic chemicals into a river. I encourage you, since you feel suffocated worshiping inside a church building, to pray outside in the original cathedral of adoration. Be patient as you strive to reclaim your ancestral prehistoric gift of sensing the awesome presence of God in nature. Let each of the four seasons be your four gospels, and be inspired by the first word of God made flesh—creation.

In our phone conversation I referred to you as an Exodus
Christian. As such you will feel the tension of being suspend-
ed between what you've left behind and what is yet to come.
Exodus Christians are road people, spiritual gypsies, so be prepared to be forced to wander for years in the desert as did those
people of the First Exodus. I encourage you to trust that you'll
not starve because, just as God rained down on them manna
from heaven, so too will God feed you in mysterious ways.

The Teacher Jesus compared his instructions to that heavenly manna bread by declaring that his spiritual food never goes
stale. I suggest you practice daily or frequent spiritual reading
for your nourishment as a pilgrim on the road, even though I
dislike the adjective "spiritual" since it seems to imply that our
spirit exists somehow apart from the rest of our person. Reading
nourishes the soul as does worship. Trust that your thirst will
be quenched in the bottomless well of the New Testament, but
I propose using a cup (and not a bucket) and sipping slowly
what you read.

We live in a new cosmic reality where Earth is no longer the
center of the universe, and this requires a stretching of all our
horizons, so expand your scriptural reading beyond the Bible.
Today bookstores hold the rich treasure of excellent English
translations of the religious texts of all the world's great religions. Whenever you read a passage in one of them that speaks
truth or calls you to holiness, you will know those words—
regardless of their source—were inspired by the Holy Spirit.
Also available today is a vast array of books on spirituality,
prayer, and reflections on the gospels. Find an author or authors who speak to you, and begin the daily practice of reading
a short passage from one of their books. I say books in the plural

since you best nourish your inner life with readings taken from a large pantry rich in a variety of writings.

Finally I conclude by encouraging you to not only "keep the faith" but also to increase it, even if your living out of that faith isn't that of your parents or relatives. Thomas Jefferson said each new generation would be a new republic, and the same is true with religion. Each new generation will be a new and different faith expression. I wish you peace, both of heart and spirit, and encourage you take heart by knowing that you are not alone. The vast majority of believers feel as alienated as do you, and even if they are unknown to you, they are companion gypsies of faith traveling the exodus road.

Letter to Eileen
About Freedom in Prayer and Hypocrisy

Dear Eileen,

I appreciated your letter in response to mine after our reunion lunch some weeks ago. And I am pleased to respond to your struggle to resolve the meaning of common expressions like "to pray." You wrote that when we say "pray," we only mean we hope or wish for a successful resolution of some pressing need or event, like your brother-in-law Jack's critical heart surgery. Since I've known you, I've been aware that even while you've been religiously inclined, you've struggled with questions about who or what is God. I recall you wrestling with these same questions forty years ago when I taught you as a high school student, and I understand your prayer predicament when God is perceived as an unfathomable mystery, some impenetrable question mark.

The act of praying raises the question: "Is anyone listening to my prayer, or am I just talking to myself?" Or, you ask, "How could anyone, even a supernatural being, lovingly listen to my private small petitions when an entire world wracked with woe is screaming for help? How could God be concerned about the ghastly horrors of countries at war, a plague laying waste to an entire people, or the starvation of thousands, and yet find time to be concerned about my trivial individual issues?" Those who truly stop and seriously question as do you are usually buried in an avalanche of questions. Before acknowledging the real dilemma of your questions, I want to congratulate you on being question-bound, since that state places you in a holy and fruitful place. Privileged are those who are brave enough to wrestle with God, for they shall be granted an abundance of rich blessings!

Prayers are addressed to God, a Mystery better conceived as Spirit. So consider addressing your prayers to the Spirit of love, the Spirit of healing or encouragement, or whatever gift is needed. Primary is the Spirit of Love, radioactive in an intense energy capable of instantly telescoping time and space. Whenever we remember anyone in prayer, especially someone we love, I believe that a subtle, powerful energy force surrounds and touches that person. To simply think with love of another person is to pray for them. Whenever in the midst of the activities of your day you become aware that you are thinking of someone, living or dead, you are praying for them. All of life is one vast interconnected web; everything and everyone is intimately linked together. Whenever you remember someone with love or in prayer, or even if only in thought, you caress a strand of the sacred web that causes the entire web-work to vibrate, and connects you with everyone and everything.

Paul, writing a letter to the early Christians in Rome (Rom 8:26–27), says we should let go of worrying if we know how to pray and simply let the Spirit express with unimaginable beauty our groaning and yearning for those who are in need. The great news is to stop worrying and let the Holy Spirit be your prayer-spokesperson—and your spiritual counselor. You wrote of your concerns that if you no longer attend church, how will God speak to you? Paul says that the Spirit within you will speak to you of God and those things you need to hear. While I hope you will find these words encouraging, they do not diminish your questions about what words to use when you pray, since the old prayers you learned now seem archaic and insufficient.

Recently an old friend, who, like you, is also an Exodus Christian, wrote me a letter about prayer. He began it by quoting a book he was reading entitled *Surpassing Wonder* by Donald Harmen Akenson: "In linguistics, language is not merely a reproducing system for voicing ideas, but is a shaper of ideas. The words not only express ideas, but shape them." He went on in his letter to further quote Akenson, "One of the great vanities of human beings is that they have ideas. Little ideas maybe, but when it comes to the big idea, it is the ideas that have people." My friend wrote of how both he and I are believers in God, but the words that shape our expressions of that belief are unique to each of us. He finds the idea of God to be a dynamic and progressively changing idea and so wonders if his prayer should also be the same.

Indeed, the words of our prayers are extremely important, as they are continuously shaping our ideas about God and the church. Words shape our consciousness, and so the institutional church rigidly controls the prayers and rituals of worship. They insist upon the use of precise words in the prayers of worship, since these words shape the ideas of the faithful about both the church and God. Typically, the words in the official prayers of the church narrowly restrict and limit those who belong to the Body of Christ to only those of a particular church. Also, the required liturgical prayer of the eucharistic liturgy is a pyramid prayer that—by beginning at the pinnacle and then descending—reinforces hierarchical order.

The memorized prayers of our youth are the ones most frequently used, as they more easily come to our lips. Other than the Lord's Prayer, before you pray any of these old traditional prayers, examine them to see if the words you pray are in conflict with your present ideas about how you see yourself in relationship to God. An example taken from the language of prayers of previous times: Do you really feel like a wretched sinner who must plead for mercy? If not, don't pray that way. What I've said about prayers is equally true for the words of hymns and songs of worship. They also are potent shapers of ideas and are not insignificant in how you image God.

Hypocrisy in prayer—be it recited or sung—is to use pious words that are devoid of honest intention or real desire. For example, for a white, Anglo-Saxon, middle-class parish congregation to zealously sing "Come Holy Spirit!" is to call down upon themselves the Great Holy Disturber, the Status-Somersaulting Whirlwind of God. Would anyone in their right mind passionately urge the Spirit to descend upon them and radically turn their lives upside down as it did the life of Mary of Nazareth, the prophets of Israel, or the apostles? Likewise, examine your prayers of petition for the presence of hypocrisy or idle pious wishes. Such empty prayer-wishes can be prayers of petition for the needs of the poor that are impotent to move those who pray them to actually go out and do something concrete for the needy.

Often the words of our prayers are more for our comfort and sense of communion with God. Prayers should rather be springboards to catapult us into being more compassionate toward the poor, more patient with those with whom we work and live, and non-judgmental. The bottom line is my encouragement to pray less, but more honestly, by praying only those words you truly believe. When you are praying with others or in a church ritual, be prepared to experience prayer-lapses, seconds of silence where you skip over words that express ideas or beliefs you can't honestly pray or sing.

So in conclusion, I repeat to always pray as honestly as you can, even if that means you find yourself praying less. It is my belief that all of us are in for a gigantic surprise after we die: God will praise us for all the times in life that we prayed—those times and places that, without us knowing it, we were praying. Prayer is more than words; it's a living communion with the Sacred Mystery. May the Holy Spirit, who saturated Jesus in his prayer times—the same Spirit who also dwells within you—saturate your prayers with holy authenticity.

First Letter to Richard
About Living the Faith in Exile

Dear Richard,

In setting a time for our lunch and conversation, I remarked that the day would be the second Wednesday in Lent. Knowing you were no longer attending church, I realize I had slipped back into viewing time according to a religious calendar. You interrupted my apology saying that you had been conscious that last Wednesday was Ash Wednesday, and we then had a brief discussion about the importance of sacred time. This letter is a follow-up of that exchange and also a preface to our upcoming luncheon conversation in which we agreed to discuss the issue of how non-church-attending Christians relate to their former religious calendar. The other day I read an essay that lamented the loss of the ability of people to celebrate holidays in our contemporary workaholic world. The author, Barbara Ehrenreich, said that in fifteenth-century France, one out of four days of the year was set aside for celebrations that usually centered on saints' days and other religious feasts. The religious cycle of feasts and fasts ritualized time and gave it meaning.

You are unfortunately no longer a functioning priest, having chosen a higher vocation of marriage. We both are aware that the two sacraments of ordination and marriage do not exclude one another except in our Roman tradition. Someday old Rome, who moves slowly because she wears monstrously heavy, large leaden shoes, will return to the apostolic tradition of a married clergy. Today, we can only hope and pray that she soon gets a new pair of shoes! Because of your seminary scriptural studies, I know that you are aware of the Babylonian Captivity of the Jews, but allow me a brief review of that seeming disaster

that actually gave birth to a renewed Judaism. The Babylonian
Exile after the Exodus is the second greatest historical event in
the shaping of the Jewish faith. After capturing Jerusalem in
587 B.C., the Babylonian army leveled the city to the ground—
including the temple—and then deported a large number of
Jews to Babylon. After the destruction of their temple, which
had been the heart of their worship, the Jews dispersed outside
of Palestine.

While their worship of God had previously been exclusively centered in the temple and its rituals, now that this holy place
was in ruins, they were forced to creatively evolve new ways to
express their faith while they were in exile. These Jews in exile
continued to observe their faith while living in an alien land,
instructing their children in the faith and continuing their religious traditions while they celebrated the holy day observances
in their homes. They also came together in small gatherings that
they called a synagogue, meaning "assembly for prayer and
study of scripture." These assemblies later gave their name to
the buildings in which they were held. When the Babylonian
Captivity ended and the Jews were allowed to return to their
homes, these exile houses of prayer became an established part
of Jewish life and were found in every Palestinian town.

While this Babylonian deportation of so many into exile
could have signaled the end of the Jewish people, instead their
exile became the source of beautiful and great prophetic writings and psalm prayers. So along with the Exodus, the Exile can
also be a powerful religious metaphor for what is happening to
the Christian church today.

You have expressed before to me your feelings of alienation when attending worship in the parish, so besides being
an Exodus Christian, you are also an Exile Christian. You feel

estranged from the ritual of Mass that once was extremely rich and meaningful for you. As an exile, even if you haven't been physically deported from your religious homeland, you have been theologically and liturgically displaced. I propose that a good guide for how to live out your faith in this condition of exile would be to imitate those deported Jews in Babylon and make your home your place of worship. Also, as did they, use opportunities to assemble for prayer and reflection with like-minded friends. Just as we have a New Testament, perhaps the coming years will witness the appearance of New Synagogues.

I also encourage you to continue, as did the Jews in exile, to celebrate the liturgical cycle of seasons, such as Lent or Advent, and the various holy days of the year, but in a new and non-church or sanctuary manner. By this awareness and celebration, you continue to ritualize and give meaning to time. This especially applies to making Sundays special days in the week. This weekly observance of the pivotal day of the week is an important part of ritualizing time. Your Sunday observance could be leisure time for reading, reflecting on the scriptures that are used that Sunday at church, or a special meal like brunch. Scriptural scholars say that at the time of Jesus, attendance at the synagogue on Saturday wasn't mandatory. Common folk kept the Sabbath holy simply by resting and leisure, so if that becomes your ritual pattern, know that you're in good company by imitating the Master. Make these Sunday activities into sacred rituals by repetition of routines or activities and by the consciousness that God saturates all space and time.

Give my love to your wife. I look forward to seeing you and to our conversation at lunch next Wednesday.

Second Letter to Richard
About Being an Exile Christian

Dear Richard,

Greetings to you and your brothers and sisters in exile. It is my hope that you will read this letter at your next gathering since it continues our discussion about how you and those who gather with you for prayer and reflection are like the ancient Israelites who once lived exiled in Babylon. Six centuries before the birth of Jesus, the Babylonian armies leveled to the ground the city of Jerusalem and its great temple. They forced the elite and influential Israelites of the city and surrounding area into exile. You can image the great sorrow at the loss of their religion, which had sustained them for centuries—a religion centered upon the great temple in Jerusalem with its elaborate rituals and ceremonies.

Surely the Israelites must have questioned where their God was when what they loved and found so nourishing was taken away from them. You can identify with their sense of loss, as the Vatican now seems to be canceling out the dynamic springtime renewal that immediately followed the Second Vatican Council—that new style of church, giving laity their rightful roles, creative eucharistic liturgies, and real ecumenism with other Christian churches. Those once hopeful days of new life for the faith are now gone, and you sense profoundly being in exile as once again clericalism reigns in many corners, interfaith dialogue and ecumenism have largely evaporated, and those hope-filled dreams of a new church seem to have been aborted.

The sorrow of being exiled while remembering the former times was vividly expressed by the Hebrew psalmist in Psalm

137, who today gives voice to your grief and that of countless others like you:

> By the rivers of Babylon, we sat mourning and
>   weeping
> when we remembered Zion.
> On the willows of that land we hung our harps.
> There our captors asked us for the words of a
>   song . . . a joyful song.
> But how could we sing a song of the Lord in a
>   foreign land?

A contemporary form of that ancient Psalm could be:

> By the front doors of church we sit mourning
>   and weeping
> as we remember the former days of springtime
>   renewal.
> We weep at the loss of creative liturgies that
>   once spoke to us in our own
> language of our communion with the poor and
>   dispossessed,
> of our mission for peace and justice.
> The clergy ask us to sing joyful songs about the
>   church,
> but how can we—whom they have sent into
>   exile—
> sing joyfully in a foreign church?

The typical response I encounter from disenfranchised Catholic Christians is that of the sorrow of loss, which is understandable. That's if what has and is happening to your institutional religion is viewed in a strictly secular or historical way. If you judge the present situation in the Church in a purely

Letter to Paula and Her Friends Who Gather at Her Home

Dear Paula and Friends,

I am writing to you in this letter about a commonly used word that has radical implications—church—because "the Church" has presented such problems for you and your friends. Be patient as I review with you the meanings in this common term. The English word *church* comes from the Scottish *kirk* and German *kirche*, which owe their origins to the late Greek *kyriakon*, meaning "the Lord's house." While clearly implying a building, the broader meaning of a community of believers is from another Greek word, *ekklesia*. This was a secular word in classical Greek used for an assembly of the citizens of a city for the purpose of passing laws or deliberation. The writers of the Greek scriptures adopted the secular Greek *ekklesia* to express the Hebrew *kahal*, meaning a religious assembly of the Israelites, which in the New Testament first appears as *Kahal Yahweh*, "the religious assembly of God." The word *kahal* also signified Moses' desert band of the Exodus Israelites, and so in the gospels when Jesus uses the word *church* for his small band of followers, he would have been thinking of a kahal.

Since the days of the Vatican Council in the early 1960s, the word *church* was very often translated as "the People of God" or "the Body of Christ." The transition from centuries of thinking of the Church as a hierarchical institution governed by bishops and the pope, or a local community governed by a board of elders, to that of the People of God required a major shift in consciousness. That transition back to the concept of the ancient kahal as a definition of what it means to belong to a church continues to this day, as you and your friends know from personal experience. I want to return to this historical and critical evolution of religious consciousness later in this letter, but for your prayerful reflection I ask you to consider the implications contained in the original Greek *ekklesia*, literally meaning "called out."

It means not summoned out to debate some civil issue but rather to a fundamental life change. Wes Howard-Brook in his book *The Church Before Christianity* writes that the Greek *ekklesia* expresses how the spirit of the risen Jesus has called his followers out of the world to live as an alternative community. In this, the beginning decades of the twenty-first century, does being church, *ekklesia*, mean to be called out of the institutional structure to be new witnesses to the alternative community of the Risen One? If so, have you and your group of women friends, who say you have left the Church, truly left, or have you become the church, the "called out" ones? The Second Vatican Council document on mission *(Ad Gentes)* begins its first chapter with these words: "The pilgrim church is missionary by her very nature." The gospels don't come after the Church; they precede it—and the Church only appears when those who are church are proclaiming the gospel as a way of life.

Having suffered frustration after frustration, sterile worship, and feeling excluded by the language used when you attend church, you no longer attend except for rare occasions such as weddings or funerals. I encourage you, however, to discuss together this possibility: Can you be "called out" of the institutional Church while also remaining within it? If this is possible, what are the implications for you and for the Church?

TWO

Letters to the
Christian Churches
of the Exodus

Letter to the Gatherings of Exodus Christians in Denver on "Keeping the Faith"

Dear Brothers and Sisters of the Faith,

This letter is addressed not only to you, but also to all Exodus Christians in whatever cities they dwell. The subject of this letter is that old Irish expression used when saying goodbye to someone, "Keep the faith." It is not heard as often today as it once it was, but perhaps now is the time for that expression to have a resurrection. I've often wondered if it may have originated as a farewell in Ireland in the mid-nineteenth century during the time of the great migration to America. "Keep the faith" would have been a natural parting wish for family and friends departing for a predominantly Protestant country where their Catholic faith would be tested and easily lost since they would be a maligned and discriminated minority. "Keep the faith" could be a blessing-farewell today, when six or seven out of ten Christians no longer attend church on a regular basis.

The expression may have flowed from attending the baptisms of their own children, or those of family members, where the ritual began with the priest asking the infant's parents, "What dost thou ask of the Church of God?" Their or the godparents' answer to that question was known by heart and spoken with force: "Faith!" Faith is a gift. It is a gift given by God to an adult prior to seeking entrance into the church and a precious inherited gift parents give to their children. To be gifted with faith is not to be given some abstract concept but a way of life, a moral compass, a membership in a community of companion believers, and a pledge of life beyond this one of toil and pain. To safeguard one's faith was critical for those leaving the tight network of their families, the security of small villages and a countryside where that religious faith was the most precious possession of those who lived constantly on the precipice of destitution and starvation.

America is the land of immigrants. Regardless of our immigrant heritage, be it Polish, German, Italian, Spanish, or Asian, be it Lutheran, Catholic, Presbyterian, or Methodist, our ancestors each came to the shores of this country carrying the treasure of their religious faith. In order to keep the faith, they gravitated toward living in the same ethnic areas of large cities or settled in small farming communities and villages of people who were predominately of their faith. Faith feeds and is sustained by being surrounded by those who share it, even if that religious faith may in certain cases be more a national identity or family tradition than a living belief.

Now at the beginning of this twenty-first century, a century and a half later, "keep the faith" has once again become a blessing safeguard wish, a prayerful hope that is extended to brother and sister Exodus Christians who no longer desire to attend the weekly services of their own faith communities.

Spiritual writers all reinforce the necessity of a faith community. That seems to imply the requirement of belonging and attending a parish church. Yet Jesus says the only community needed for him to be present is when two or three of his disciples came together in his name! That only two persons are sufficient to make a community is reinforced by the post-resurrection account in Luke's Gospel of the two disciples on the road to Emmaus. When at their sunset meal they break bread with a stranger whom they have invited to dine with them, they recognize in him the mystical presence of their Risen Christ. Luke's Gospel presents us with the Emmaus Sacrament not only as an image of how only the presence of a few is required to have church, but also as an alternate Eucharist that is possible for the non-ordained at any table or meal.

Today, clergy preach that to maintain your faith, weekly attendance at Sunday worship and reception of Holy Communion is absolutely necessary. While weekly worship, prayer, and Holy Communion can be an exceedingly rich source of strength and affirmation of one's faith, that these are "absolutely necessary" is questionable. A personal story will illustrate that there are other means than weekly church attendance to keep the faith.

My grandfather was the son of Irish immigrants, and my father was born on a farm in western Nebraska at the end of the nineteenth century. The closest Catholic church to their prairie farmstead was in the distant town of York, which required a four- to five-hour wagon ride to reach. Attending Sunday Mass meant the hardship of traveling half a day in an open wagon to reach church, and then an hour for Mass followed by a basket lunch. To return home after attending church meant repeating that long wagon ride back to their home, which required the rest of the entire day. As a result of the hardship, especially in winter and bad weather, my father told me the family attended church perhaps only four times a year. Even without weekly worship, this Irish farm family of five girls and a boy maintained a strong religious faith for their entire lives!

A hundred years ago Holy Communion was typically received only once a year, usually on Easter or some Sunday in the fifty days of Eastertide, yet that was sufficient to keep the faith. So, lacking frequent Communion and weekly worship, by what means did they keep their faith? Besides my grandparents teaching their children the basics of their religious faith, they led them in praying daily meal prayers, and each night they prayed the rosary together. Years later, when my father's parents moved to a farm just outside of York, they and their teenage children attended Mass weekly.

This personal story demonstrates the possibility of nourishing your religious faith with only a minimum of church worship and reception of the sacraments if there is a living faith and prayer in the home. So I encourage you as Exodus Christians to maintain the practice of prayer at the table, one of the most ancient of prayer times, as well as at other times. If presently you do not pray before meals, consider beginning with some ritual action or words. Keeping the faith, as that hundred-years-ago story demonstrates, is possible when you create a home church where parents perform the priestly duties of blessings and being the family prayer leaders. I have visited some homes where parents have a child lead the meal prayers, but I feel this sends the wrong message that religion is for children. Since the most ancient times, the patriarchs and matriarchs were recognized as being invested with the divine power of blessing. Parents are the priests, the pastors, of the home church, and it is they who should be the family prayer leaders. Today, just as many parents have chosen to home school their children, the time is long overdue for many to be home churched.

Letter to Exodus Assemblies of Sioux Falls on the Holy Exodus Spirit as a Guide in Your Faith Life

Dear Exodus Pilgrim People,

In the 1960s the Second Vatican Council used the description "The Pilgrim People of God" for the Christian faithful, and unknowingly their use of this new name was prophetic. Not only does that title express the concept of being on a life journey as a member of the New Exodus, it is a reminder that Christians live an illusion if they believe that by belonging to the church, they have arrived. Pilgrim people are perpetual travelers, even if they never leave home. While it is our custom to refer to the deceased as "departed," I understand that in parts of Africa they speak of those who have died as "having arrived." Indeed, only in death does the journey end.

Today, over forty years after that historic Council, a majority of Catholics have now indeed become pilgrims, not lost wanderers, but sojourners inspired and guided by the Holy Spirit. As sojourners of the Spirit, I encourage you to be vigilant in keeping the faith as you anticipate that day in the distant future when your church undergoes the radical transformation seeded in it by that Vatican Council. Be open to allowing the Spirit of discernment to guide you in finding a worshiping faith community that speaks to your heart and nourishes your soul, even if it happens to be another denomination. The Teacher said that in heaven God had many mansions, and since the Reformation, that is also true here on earth.

I have a good friend who faithfully attends Mass each Saturday night, and then on Sunday morning he accompanies his wife, who is a devout Presbyterian, to worship in her church.

He asked me if he could remain a Catholic and also apply for membership in his wife's Presbyterian church, since their creed of belief required for membership is the same as his. He echoed what I have heard from others, saying he sensed more in his wife's church that spoke to his heart and nourished his soul. He experienced a stronger sense of belonging to a community in his wife's church than he did in his own parish, and wanted to be both a Catholic and a Presbyterian. I replied that if he felt he would be more a part of that worshiping community of believers and experienced the presence of God with them, then why not officially become a member? I compared the situation to dual citizenship, such as Canadian and American, or like being a member of the church of Corinth and also a member of the church of Ephesus, since we are baptized into Christ, not into this or that church.

I conclude this letter about following the Spirit of Truth by encouraging you to let that Spirit lead you to places that you never before thought possible. The Spirit will guide each of you, as it has my good friend, to find creative solutions to your quest for worship, community, and spiritual growth. The Spirit has as many names as there are gifts, and so I pray that the Spirit of Tenacity will help each of you to remain steadfast in the midst of your religious struggles to keep the faith.

Letter to the Faithful of the Lake Street House, Who Gather in Friendship, Reflection on Scripture, and Celebrations of the Lord's Supper

Dear Companions of the Faith
gathered at the Lake Street House,

I greet you with peace as you once again come together to meet as a small community of faith and friendship. Some of you are married, others of you are now single, and while you come from different professions and family backgrounds, you all share a common feeling of being alienated from the church. Outwardly you would appear to be only a book club since the core of your communal evenings is a discussion about a book you are jointly reading. But that exchange of reflections on what you've read is only a beginning for your deeper exchange of stories of your lives, your faith, and the sharing of a holy and festive potluck dinner.

I understand that before you eat your meal, you have a prayer service. Men and women take turns leading your communal prayer, and part of that period of prayer is the Last Supper ritual of the breaking of bread and the sharing of a cup of wine. While some could object or even condemn this last sacred ritual of your gatherings, are you not being faithful to the command of Jesus to "do this in memory of me"? He didn't restrict who among his disciples could remember him by this table ritual. The followers of the risen Jesus met in private homes in the early, post-resurrection church and, as was and is now household custom, the host or hostess presided at a meal. So it became the accepted practice that the host or hostess in whose home the followers gathered would preside at the memorial meal.

While few in number, those early Christians found hope and support from each other in their clandestine celebrations of the Jesus Supper in their private homes. More than two millennia later, you Exodus Christians are now following in their apostolic footsteps as you faithfully gather at the home on Lake Street to sustain and deepen your faith.

However, I encourage you to follow the wisdom of the Master, who cautioned, "Be cunning as serpents and as innocent as doves." Be like the first Christians and continue to keep your celebrations of the Jesus Supper clandestine. Some Christians would be scandalized by your actions, and the clergy surely would denounce and condemn your fidelity to observing the command of Jesus, "Do this in memory of me."

In the earliest days of the apostolic church, the leader of the Memorial Meal of Jesus was usually the head of the house. If the house where they gathered belonged to a widow, then she led the ritual of the Jesus Supper as their hostess. Since baptism was viewed as full incorporation into Christ, they believed that every baptized Christian, male or female, was empowered to baptize, forgive sins, and break bread. As the numbers of believers increased, the role of who should preside at the eucharist slowly shifted away from the head of the house to certain specified elders of the larger community. Later on it evolved into today's ordained clergy.

I understand that many in your group continue to go to church on Sundays, and that is admirable, knowing how you usually find it less than nourishing. I support the spiritually healthy balance that you've created by remaining part of the larger church by your Sunday attendance, as well as by living and nourishing your faith by your monthly small community prayer gatherings.

Your continued parish involvement each week reminds you that you belong to the whole Body of Christ: aged and young, politically conservative and liberal, known friends and strangers, those eager for radical change in the church and those eager to go back to what it was like forty years ago.

One of the dangers of small household communities of faith is that they can easily become gatherings of the like-minded instead of those who, as Paul said, "take on the mind of Christ" (1 Cor 2:16). Such a Christ-mind transplant re-creates you to think inclusively; removes all social, racial, and sexual barriers; and makes you like-hearted with Christ.

I encourage you also in your prayerful ritual of the Jesus Supper to include in your petitionary prayers the needs of countless other small clandestine communities like yours, not only here in America but also across the globe. While those gathered there on Lake Street are only a small handful, you are but one church (and you are a church as it was defined in the early days of Christianity) in a vast network of small communities of faith. Presently you feel unconnected, even anonymous, and thus isolated, but that is not the reality. Covering the world is a vast, sacred web composed of companion seekers and faith communities, even some as small as only two or three. Remind yourselves of this whenever your community celebrates the Jesus Meal, and pray so that the entire invisible sacred web vibrates with energy.

On the issue of your communal prayers, I encourage you to pray for the global institutional Church, along with its bishops and pastors. While often their superior attitudes and uncompassionate moral declarations cause you irritation and even anger, remember that they sincerely believe in their vision of the Church. They genuinely believe that the strict laws of how to worship and the rigid regulations of how to live the gospel are the right way for them and, sadly, that these are also the way that you should live. They need your prayers and compassion since it is fear and not love that guides their judgments and decisions. Love and prayer unite; ideology and theology too often divide. If we have truly taken on the mind of Christ, then we cannot think in terms of "them" and "us," for we are all one.

I conclude this letter with my prayers for the continued success of your apostolic endeavor. I seal this letter with the hope that you will continue to find nourishment and encouragement as you gather for conversation and to share the Jesus Supper. Take heart in the historical reality that your gatherings at Lake Street House are a reflection and a continuation of the ancient apostolic church, as well as being a beautiful mirror of the emerging future church.

Letter to the Exodus Churches of Savannah Concerning the Gospel Sacraments and the Body of Christ

Dear Loyal Exodus Believers of Savannah,

This letter is to encourage you and to affirm that you are not separated from the body of Christ by your inability to identify yourself as Christians who worship faithfully each week. The body of Christ is larger than any individual church, regardless of how apostolic or orthodox it may claim to be. I write to encourage you to be vigilant and not be tempted to satisfy your God-hunger with empty foods offered by the false gods of the marketplace.

I also encourage you to be wary of honky-tonk religion offered by groups or churches that feed on people's desire for spectacular entertainment in worship services, akin to show business. If you hunger for the spectacular, feed that desire in the rightful place—the theater. Be even more cautious of falling prey to multitude mysticism, the exhilaration of finding yourself being engulfed in an ocean of believers at some massive religious event, since such grand services only give illusionary testimony to the vitality of religion. Apparently, some believers need to have their personal faith buoyed up by attending religious gatherings in large stadiums jammed with co-believers or by worshipping in crowded, mammoth-sized churches.

Some, in their attempt to fill the void left in their lives after leaving institutional religion, turn to New Age spiritualities. The exercises of these contemporary spiritualities tend to focus on personal health, self-fulfillment, and various methods of relaxation. They usually avoid the negative (and therefore unpleasant) issues, such as poverty, exploitation of the weak, and other social injustices. Instead, they promote thinking only positive thoughts, the use of herbal aromas, or the power of healing crystals.

Instead of New Age spiritualities, I propose you seriously explore Old Age spiritualities. By "old" I refer to those spiritualities of the apostolic, early pre-clerical, non-hierarchical church. The practice of apostolic, old age spirituality offers to ritualistic persons like yourselves the rich nourishment of the gospel sacraments. As you remember, the sacraments of the Church are outward signs of an inward grace instituted by Christ for the individual's sanctification. Some Christian churches have seven, while others distinguish between greater and lesser sacraments. Regardless of the number, both the sacraments of the Church and the sacraments of the gospel are valid sources of grace. The gospel sacraments as channels of grace were also instituted by Christ and today are the sacraments that support and nourish the faith of those who no longer attend church, along with those who do.

We begin with the first and chief gospel sacrament, the Emmaus Sacrament. It is the common, shared meal as a living extension of the Church's sacrament of the Lord's Supper or the celebration of the eucharist. This graced act at a table is experienced outside of church walls in the commonplace mealtimes of friendship and family. A prayer of blessing, a toast, or some silent ritual like breaking and sharing a piece of bread is a way to acknowledge the sacredness of a graced meal. This gospel table sacrament is named after the Easter event in Luke's gospel where the two disciples at the village of Emmaus shared an ordinary meal with a stranger. As they broke the bread at that meal, their eyes were opened and they recognized that the stranger was the risen Jesus. Paradoxically, in today's Emmaus

These seven are only some of the gospel sacraments, so I encourage you as you read the gospels and prepare to discover other gospel channels of grace. Peace and blessings to each of you personally and all those of your small Exodus community of believers. Finally, rejoice that you, as a gathering or community of the faithful, regardless of how small your numbers, are a sacrament of the gospel!

Letter to Exodus Christians of Albuquerque About Finding the Forgiveness of Christ for Your Sins and Failings

Dear Friends and Believers in Christ the Healer,

I have sent to you a copy of my letter to your sister and brother Exodus Christians of Savannah concerning celebrating the sacraments of ordinary life that do not require the presence of ordained clergy. In this letter I would like you to reflect on the gospel sacrament of the forgiveness of sins. In the pardoning of others and in being pardoned yourself, this is perhaps the most frequent of all sacred household exchanges. Since it is the most frequently administered household sacrament, I am making it the subject of an entire letter.

We are imperfect humans and not angels; intentional or accidental mistakes, offenses, and misunderstandings are part of the very fabric of domestic life, thus making necessary this healing sunset sacrament. The sacrament-maker Jesus, being aware of the "being rubbed the wrong way" realities of daily life, insisted that we never let the sun set on our anger. In both the Roman and Episcopal churches this sacrament of being pardoned is called *confession* or *reconciliation* when penitents ritually confess their sins to a priest. After a brief exhortation, the priest then pronounces a prayer of pardon over the person. This face-to-face confession, as is common today, or the faceless confession in the darkness of a confessional hold great healing powers for removing guilt and shame and obtaining the reassurance of the approval of the all-seeing God.

So universal is this human need for confession that in the later part of the twentieth century, an enterprise appeared of a pay-by-the-minute telephone confession. For a slight charge, people could anonymously confess their guilt-burdening sins of marital infidelity, larceny, or lying—not by confessing to a priest, but to a total stranger who would listen to their confessions. The customers of this service were either Roman Catholics who no longer confessed to a priest or members of other Christian churches, along with non-believers who simply felt a deep need to anonymously confess their moral failings to another human. Confession is good for the soul, or so it has been said.

When you are aware of having caused pain to another, you have an obligation, Jesus the sacrament-maker said, to go to that person and ask him or her to forgive you. After asking pardon, the offended person then has a sacred obligation to grant pardon and forgiveness to the offender. In this exchange of pardon and peace, the two persons enter into a unity with each other and with Christ that is truly a living holy communion.

From my discussions with other Exodus Christians, I am aware that for most of you it has been many years since you confessed to a priest, and in this you are not alone. Recent surveys have shown that you are among over 50 percent of Catholics who do not go to confession even once a year! Another 20 to 30 percent go only once or twice a year. Like you, they are good people striving to do their best each day and not unrepentant, public sinners self-blinded to their grievous faults. You, like these countless others, having failed to find in yourself any terrible sin grave enough to require confessing, tend to feel guilty for not feeling guilty! I rejoice that you have been given the grace to refuse to be shamed by old echoes of a conscience formed many years ago and in another age. Be confident in following your presently formed conscience that tells you your small failings have not separated you from the love of God.

Be prepared, however, that the clergy can point an accusing finger at this lack of going to confession and denouncing it as another sign of today's decadent decline in morality. If you attend church on Ash Wednesday or during Lent, be prepared to hear the clergy remind you, along with their parishioners, that the confession of sins to a priest at least once a year at Eastertide has been a requirement of the Church for almost a thousand years. Confession at least once a year—but not necessarily to a priest—is like an annual medical check up and a good practice.

You are not a notorious sinner, but you may still have a need for pardon and absolution. If you have this hunger for pardon, and for whatever reason do not wish to engage in a church ritual, I suggest that you take seriously the teaching of St. Augustine on the forgiveness of sins. This holy bishop of the fourth century and brilliant theologian, Augustine, told his newly baptized converts that if they stumbled and sinned, they could find pardon for their sins by simply praying the Lord's Prayer with faith. Pray slowly with deep faith the prayer that Jesus gave his disciples, especially these words: " . . . and forgive us our sins/trespasses, as we forgive those who trespasses/sin against us." Augustine took Jesus at his word when he said, "Ask and it will be granted to you," and you should do the same.

So, friends and faithful believers, I conclude by wishing each of you and those you love the gifts of peace, tranquility, and serenity as you strive daily to live the high ideals of the Way of Jesus. Let your every fall and failure become a fertile occasion for you to arise, dust yourself off, and strive to live with even more zeal and love.

Letter to the Exodus Christians of Pittsburgh on the Impossibility of Being Excommunicated from the Love of God

Dear Faithful Brothers and Sisters,

If I were to sum up in a single sentence all that is needed for you to remain faithful to the will of God as a non-church-attending Christian, it would sound too easy, too simplistic. Yet everything that is truly needed for you can be encapsulated in this two-word formula: "Love God." One of the first Exodus Christians, Paul of Tarsus—who also felt impelled by the Spirit of God to find his spiritual fulfillment outside of the legalism of his birth religion of Judaism—can be your apostolic spiritual director. Paul didn't cease being a Jew or renounce his religion of birth, but instead became a Messianic Jew who made as his new rule of life the teachings of Jesus.

Each of you who, like him, are seeking a fuller expression of your religious faith should take encouragement in his words: "We know that all things work for the good of those who love God" (Rom 8:28). "All things" can mean many things and can include the anxiety of being spiritually adrift without the assuring approval of Holy Mother Church. It can also mean dealing with religious confusion, guilt, and feelings of rejection, as Paul did.

Churches tend to indoctrinate their members with a survivalist, lifeboat mentality, telling them things like, "Outside of the Church there is no salvation." So it can be ominously intimidating for you to choose to leave the lifeboat in order to swim on your own in the threatening sea of life. "Fear not," Exodus Christians, for as Paul wrote to the little house churches in the Greek city of Corinth, "If God is for us, who can be against us?"

And he goes on to say to those afraid of being condemned or excommunicated, "Who will bring an accusation against God's chosen ones? What will separate us from the love of Christ?" Then he ends with a litany of serious things that will never be able to separate us from the love of God: death, angels, earthly powers, or any creature.

You will not drown if you're helplessly cast adrift in a sea of sharks as long as you cling to that revelation of the absolute inseparability of God's love for us. Such a wondrous love requires a fantastically generous response of loving God in return with all your heart. Jesus said such a totality of loving God and neighbor—in the manner you love yourself—fulfilled all religious laws, including Sunday worship and the commandments. John Calvin would echo and expand that moral judgment of Jesus by saying that the love of God included the "whole of religion." Surely, the faithful attendance at Sunday worship and the observance of other Church laws are intended to support and encourage your love of God, but if they cease to bring you closer, then find the "whole" of your religion in simply loving God. We love God, as Jesus wisely taught, by loving our neighbors, strangers, and our enemies with the same attention we pay to our own needs.

Lovingly caring for the needs of others in your life and in the world is how we demonstrate our love of God. Everyone in the world is in need, even if only of being loved and appreciated. God is absolutely without any need, except, as Jesus taught, for one thing: our love. So, along with expressing your love of God by your concern and care for others, I encourage you to strive daily to express your love to the unspeakable, indefinable, and nameless Mystery of God.

Consider the daily habit of saying aloud, "O my Divine Beloved, I love you with all my heart and soul. Help me this day to love you with every breath I take." If you desire, expand this short prayer by adding, "May every fiber of my being, every gene in my DNA, passionately love you who has with such affection loved me into existence."

Most of us doubt, at least at times, that we are lovable and, because of our weakness, find it impossible to believe that God is passionately in love with us. As agnostics of love, we say, "Oh, I believe God loves the world, especially those chosen ones, the saints, and the good people who steadfastly go week after week to worship whether or not they get anything at all out of the service. But someone like me?" Our ears itch to hear what Jesus heard at his baptism when a voice from the clouds said, "This is my beloved, upon whom my favor rests." Today, clouds are no longer divine instruments of communication, but I assure you that, if you proclaim your love for God daily, God will respond. These divine expressions of love will be like those old letters placed in wine bottles, corked and set afloat on the sea. So the next time you receive a surprise gift on the shores of the sea of life, an expression of love, some blessing or good fortune, remove the cork and read the message.

May these tokens of love confirm that by loving God, all things—your struggles of faith, religious qualms or skepticisms, questions and dark nights of the soul—are being woven into a harmony that is holy. Blessings on all of you, and continue to keep the faith by loving God.

Letter to Exodus Christians of San Francisco on Being Hopeful in Spite of Disappointments with Your Church

Dear Brothers and Sisters,

I write to you as individuals and as you gather in your small groups to encourage you to keep the faith, regardless of the positions taken by your church toward you and in spite of your own sense of alienation. The wisdom of the book of Proverbs is worth pondering: "When there is no vision, the people perish" (Prv 29:18). Today, the faith of many is perishable. This letter is written to all those who are hungry for hope. The absence today of a viable vision for a truly contemporary and American church—that, like the early apostolic churches, is inclusive—causes a dire poverty of hope. The absence of this critical source of energy creates a sense of powerlessness that spawns depression and gloom. In the beginning years of this new century, it is not unusual for small gatherings of believers, even conversations between two or three of them, to resemble wakes where those present bemoan the sad state of the church.

I write to encourage your hope as you experience sadness and depression over the regressive state of your religion at this time in its history. The source of this disappointment is the fact that most of you are old enough to have experienced the post-Vatican II springtime of the Catholic Church that began in the mid 1960s and continued well into the next decade. Those were years of joyous creativity, vitality in worship and prayer, and genuine, enthusiastic efforts to ecumenically bridge with common worship the gap between you and your Protestant friends. The future was saturated with the hope that any day we would see a married clergy, optional celibacy, and women ordained to the priesthood. It was a time of new lay communities with apostolic programs for young adults to zealously volunteer in service to those in need. Also intoxicating was the Pentecostal new wine of the laity and clergy sharing as equals in the ministries of a church that once reserved nearly all ecclesial ministries for priests, religious brothers, and women religious.

Not all in the Church found this time to be a joyously hopefilled renaissance, since change in one's religion is always difficult. While within a few years the majority enthusiastically embraced the liturgical changes and other reforms, others rejected this new expression of their age-old faith. For various reasons they needed the reassurance of the ancient worship and the inflexible rules of the Church. They took pride and firmly believed that the Mass and regulations of the Church were unchangeable, invested with an eternal ageless validity. This was an illusion.

The reality was that, over twenty-some centuries, the church of Christ had undergone numerous changes and adaptations, and this historical reality should be a source of honest hope for us today. I say "honest hope" since there are those who offer an illusionary hope that "things will improve" and simply encourage remaining steadfast in the faith and being patient. This is a false hope based on no real evidence but only on desire. As such it can be just another illusion. Instead, to find real hope, look up at the night sky on a clear night. Look beyond the stars at a universe of 18 billion years of continuous creation and destruction that is occurring at every moment and on all levels.

Let this cosmic reality of the universe be a wellspring of hope, since today it mirrors the Church on all levels: It is likewise undergoing destruction as a necessary evolution before re-creation. An infallible law of life that reflects the cosmic law of the universe is "Everything changes; nothing remains the same." Indeed, the Church is changing, and its institutional change has been slowly unfolding for the past two centuries, beginning among believers in Europe and now here in the United States, particularly since the end of the twentieth century. This evolutionary change is escalating daily, as studies about the decrease in church attendance and lack of support of the Church's moral teachings show.

Many of the clergy and some theologians perceive this change in how the faithful view their Church and its teachings as an erosion of belief. They condemn modern agnostic philosophies, self-indulgence, and the lax morals of the Western world as the cause of this breakdown in religious commitment. But what if these events in Europe, America, and elsewhere in the world are not a breakdown, but rather a breaking-through in Christianity, the necessary deterioration of an expression of faith that is no longer viable? The aged forms of Christianity, so westernized by being historically European, must by necessity collapse by breaking down if something new can break into the world. For the new to come, the old must go!

So find honest hope in the words of that insightful German theologian Karl Rahner, who said that the Second Vatican Council was the advent of a new epoch in church history, one in which Catholicism was becoming for the first time a true world church. A historical new era does not appear instantly, but rather takes decades, even centuries, to unfold. The birth of this new age for Catholic Christians has just begun, and so you must not misread the signs of the times in the hierarchical restoration of the old forms and the clericalism of the pre-Vatican II age of the Church. We are living in a moment of great transition in the Church and are, by the grace of God, living agents of that cosmic cycle of destruction and creation. Reinforce your hope with the awareness that significant changes in ideas and behavior are the results of an evolution more than a revolution. While a revolution can ignite ideas and ideals with passion, a gradual evolution is required for these to grow into tangible realities.

Never limit the inventiveness of God to radically alter the arrival date of this new epoch in our faith, but also face fully the reality of those who presently govern the Church, and the mature age of yourselves and all those eager for change. Live not in illusion but pray to be led from the unreal to real.

In conclusion, I remind you of a gift of the Spirit needed to joyfully live in reality: bulletproof hope. I encourage you to develop an enduring faith of such deep fidelity that you may not only live, but die, in holy hope.

Second Letter to the Exodus Churches of San Francisco on the Biblical Reflections of Enduring Hope

Dear Companions of the New Exodus,

I am glad that when you gather to be church, you share my letters with the other Exodus churches in San Francisco. Know that I am pleased you are pursuing that difficult task of "being church" by your New Exodus journey. While the scripture text of the First Exodus does not mention it, surely a large number of those who were oppressed in Egypt stayed home instead of fleeing with Moses from slavery. They accepted their servitude (since it included daily bread) instead of illegally escaping into the barren desert on a dangerous and seemingly hopeless journey. Likewise, there are many who today have not joined the New Exodus, preferring to continue to attend church even if they find it spiritually unfulfilling. At the time of the First Exodus, those Hebrew pilgrims had Moses as their liberator, and in him they found hope. You, however, have no Moses! While you lack a strong prophetic leader, you do not lack a liberator or guide since you have been given the Spirit of God. Allow yourselves to be inspired by the Spirit of holiness and liberty that each of you were given in baptism, and find it the never-failing wellspring of your hope.

In my last letter I encouraged you to live in an enduring hope. It has been said that hope is only hope when the situation appears hopeless! Since you are aware that the rules and practices of the Church are in the hands of powerful men firmly confirmed to the status quo, you can easily have little if any hope of seeing significant changes in the rules or the structure of the institutional Church any time soon. That all-inclusive and accepting church you must passionately long for will most likely never appear in your lifetime! However, that reality shouldn't diminish the passion of your zeal and efforts to "be church," instead of "going to church." There's an adage, one that is a personal favorite of mine: "Anything worth giving your life for—that can be achieved in your lifetime—isn't worth giving your life for!"

I urge you again to go outside on a clear night and look up at the night sky when the gigantic shadow of the institutional Church eclipses your hopes. The stars you see are shining in yesteryear's glory. So the medieval pomp and elaborately beautiful rituals of the Vatican court, like Great Britain's royal coronations, are beautifully shining in yesteryear's glory like the luminous splendor of long dead stars. The starlight that is the subject of poetry and lovers has taken hundreds of millions of years to reach your eyes, and the fiery sources of that light self-destructed millennia ago. The story of our cosmic universe is a drama of constant destruction and creation. In A.D. 1054, Chinese and Arab astronomers witnessed a supernova so intense its blaze equaled that of 500 million suns and was visible even during the daytime. Those tenth-century astronomers did not know that what they were observing had also occurred 6300 years before. A similar explosion of a supernova occurred in 5200 B.C. when the Sumerians were first building their culture in Mesopotamia (present day Iraq). Giant supernovas, like all stars, age, die, and collapse in massive explosions that cast off creative debris from which are formed new stars and planets.

The Christian church is a mere two thousand years old! Like the giant stars, the church, institutions, and nations of this world arise to blaze forth briefly in powerful glory. After a few hundred or thousand years their power and splendor fades away as they die. The cosmic process of ever-regenerating life is witnessed in each death struggle of a star, whose fiery demise explodes with its vital fragments that give birth to new creative realities. Why should not this cosmic creative cycle of death to life be happening to your church at this moment in history? If it is, then your destiny of being alive as it begins its descent isn't to be a spectator, but rather to join with God in gathering up the fragments of the old, dying church and creatively making out of them something dynamically new and alive.

Rubbish! That is what many Christians would declare about such a silly concept of the church of Christ dying! The church teaches that, of all the institutions and kingdoms of this world, it is immortal, quoting Jesus as promising he would be with his church until the end of the world. So was Jesus mistaken, as he was about the end of the world being imminent? That reassuring promise, however, didn't specify what the shape of church would be that he would be with till the end of the time, no matter if that end was ten or ten thousand years away.

The objection of some believers that it is utterly impossible to conceive of Christianity or the church as dying, or to imagine it as dead, isn't realistic or scriptural. Did not Jesus die? Is not the core of Christian belief his death and resurrection? Why should the Christian church be excluded from experiencing in itself the traumatic and most significant occurrence in his life? Why can't the church that claims to have been founded by Jesus Christ also taste defeat, diminishment, and finally death? If Christians believe that Jesus' solemn promise of life beyond death is true, then couldn't a dead and even buried church be raised up by God, as was Jesus, to a new life with a new type of body? Resurrection isn't resuscitation of the former body but rather an entirely new creation. So, if we believe in the words of Jesus, if institutional Christianity as we recognize it today disappears in the next hundred or more years in a slow death, can't we expect the appearance of an entirely new form of Christianity?

As I have said to you previously in this letter, your destiny is to be the innovative co-creators with God of that future rebirth of Christian worship and faith. Your small gatherings of Exodus believers are the Spirit-inspired laboratories of research and explorations of the new liturgies and re-created rituals of ancient beliefs. Do not be fearful to explore untried forms of worship and prayer that express the values and symbols of your American culture.

I conclude this letter by encouraging you to keep the flame of your hope burning brightly, keeping foremost before you the vision of community, the gathering of disciples that Jesus intended his church to be. Finally, dedicate yourselves as prophetic visionaries daily laboring to create Jesus' vision of communities united in love as a reality in your personal lives, homes, and neighborhoods. As you struggle to be involved in this apostolic work, remember the words of Blessed Teresa of Calcutta: "God has not called us to be successful; God has called us to be faithful."

THREE

Letters to Christians Questioning Their Faithful Attendance

In the previous letters of this book, I conversed with Christians who themselves no longer attended church worship on a regular basis or have someone in their families who don't. The following four letters are addressed to those who, while finding it difficult, have continued to be faithful to the tradition of weekly church attendance.

For this section addressed to questioning Christians I invoke the Spirit of God.

> May the Spirit of Holy Astuteness illuminate you
> to see yourself mirrored in the spiritual
>   struggles of others
> and guide you on the right path.

Letter to Joseph,
Tempted to Become an Exodus Christian

Dear Joe,

Instead of beginning "Dear Joe," I could have written, "Dear Joe, tempted to be an Exodus Christian." I have been your spiritual companion for many years now, and recently you have shared with me your growing struggles with attending church because of your pastor's sermons and his mechanized style of worship. You said you find his sermons lacking substance, and you've grown weary of his repeated emphasis on devotions to the Virgin Mary. Added to these distresses are the negative feelings of your wife, a cradle Catholic like yourself, who accompanies you to church on Sundays. Your wife, Betty, is even more dissatisfied with her experiences at church than you are, and she doesn't hesitate to complain to you about them on the way home from. You feel certain she could easily stop attending church if it were not for your desire that the two of you attend as a couple.

Although once a week is enough religion for Betty, you clearly have a greater need for a relationship with God, which is demonstrated by your personal prayer life. Since retiring you have begun going to church two or three times a week for Mass, but question if it is really worth the effort. I want to respond to some of these religious issues in this letter.

Before I do, I repeat what I've said to you previously. I am very impressed with the depth of your personal prayer life. Even before you retired, you observed the discipline of an hour of prayer, meditation, and spiritual reading every day before going to work. You've said that this wasn't a discipline, as you experienced deep benefits from your hour of silent prayer and reflection. Since your morning rituals are so richly beneficial to you, I can understand why you question your efforts to drive to church during the week for Mass, since what you experience is often devoid of inspiration.

However, while empathizing with your frustration, I encourage you to continue attending church, even on those weekdays. Please be patient as I attempt to explain my reasoning. This advice is based on an old saying about going on a pilgrimage: "A true pilgrim returns home from the shrine enriched, yet diminished in grace and faith." That saying is rooted in the mystical reality that faith and prayer are dynamic forms of energy. The reason that pilgrims of all religions go on pilgrimage to sacred sites is to be in touch with and to absorb the mystical energies that are present at those shrines. The energy, or spiritual power, of a shrine can radiate from the residue deposit of the grace-energy of the saint or holy person connected to that particular place, and also from the wondrous divine visitation that occurred there long ago.

The capacity to feel and absorb the spiritual energy of any shrine primarily requires that the pilgrim who goes there be truly a pilgrim. Sadly, pilgrimages in this jet age often attract spiritual tourists with cameras. Being on a tour, they are in a hurry and so quickly look around the shrine, snap a few pictures, say a prayer or two, and then hurriedly depart for the next site on their tour. A true pilgrim, however, isn't in a hurry. A real pilgrim enters the holy place and waits patiently and prayerfully with an open soul. For the person who by devotional prayer and reverential waiting has been sufficiently opened to receive, the invisible sacred energies of the shrine radiate outward from its walls and flow into that person's soul. A reverse mystical action takes place when true pilgrims enter any shrine; the power of their faith, devotion, and prayer are released and absorbed into the walls, floors, and structure of that sacred site.

So the mystical energies that flow from the abounding deposit of grace of any shrine are fused with the power of the prayers, the deep faith and devotion, of countless pilgrims who perhaps for centuries have visited that shrine. It is for this reason that the older the shrine, the more powerful the sacred energy that pilgrims who go there experience. Prayerful, sensitive persons unconsciously leave behind at any shrine the powerful energy fields of their faith and prayer. Therefore, a prayerful pilgrim returns home diminished because of the spiritual energies that the shrine absorbed, and enriched because of the grace to which they were exposed.

While I'm feeling you have already guessed what I am going to propose, Joe, I will do so anyway. By your fidelity in attending your parish church, even if you personally receive little conscious emotional benefits, you are influencing with your grace-faith energy those who are worshiping with you. Each time you enter church, you unconsciously bring with you the deeply rich experiences of intimacy from your morning's meditation prayer, and this power of your prayer energy radiates out from you far beyond where you can imagine. The Master spoke of the power of faith, saying that belief held the strength to move mountains. So the strength of your faith in God, in the Sacred Mysteries taking place at the altar, along with your own personal devotional love of Christ, radiates outward from you, enriching the ancient liturgy that you are attending. It unconsciously flows out to touch those with whom you are worshiping, and even into the walls of the church.

It is spiritually beneficial that you are unaware of the depths of this mysterious energy exchange—what is flowing out of you and what you are absorbing. I say "spiritually beneficial" because, if we accept the reality of this sacred exchange but in modesty are unmindful of it, it can flow more naturally. We can then be more conscious of what we are receiving instead what we are giving. We are like spiritual dynamos who, by frequent and direct connection with the Divine Mystery, generate powerful fields of energy. Regardless of what you experience emotionally at church, if you didn't attend, the religious experiences of those who did would be lessened! And the reverse is also true for you as a man of personal prayer. Regardless of any emotional feeling of being touched or not by God, your soul is affected by the release of faith and devotional energy from those gathered there in prayer with you.

This is the reason that when you enter an empty church to quietly pray, I'm sure you experience a sense of serenity, a "Presence." Just as the walls of a shrine radiate the prayerful energy of those who have prayed there, so the walls of a church are "radioactive." They radiate the prayer energy of the sacred mysteries conducted there, the prayers of those who for years have worshiped within those walls. This being the case, a prayerfully sensitive person always enters any sacred space of worship and prayer, regardless of the religion, with reverence, even a sense of awe and never as a tourist to simply look around.

A small, private ritual that might be helpful in remembering the exchange of spiritual energies that occurs in church is to consciously but inconspicuously touch your hand to the wall of the church as you leave it. Pause ever so briefly to intentionally invest the church edifice with your love, prayer, and faith.

Knowing you all these years, Joe, I can see you smiling and shaking your head, thinking, "Beautiful as all this sounds, is such a thing as spiritual energy a reality?" Your skepticism of an invisible entity is understandable, yet we both believe in a very real, extremely powerful, unseen energy—electricity. Being influenced by our secular culture, it is as easy to dismiss as a pious flight of the imagination the possibility of an equivalent existence of spiritual energy. Recall the gospel story of the sick woman who saw Jesus the healer passing by, surrounded by a great crowd of admirers. She thought, "If I but touch the hem of his cloak, I will be healed," so she reached down and touched it, and at that instant her sickness vanished. Jesus instantly stopped, whirled around, and demanded, "Who touched me? I felt power go out from me."

I know you'll say, but that was Jesus! Don't shortchange yourself, even if all of us quite often doubt the dynamic power of our prayers and of our prayerful presence. Personally, I believe it is impossible for anyone to spend an hour each day in deep intimate communion with God in silent prayer, as you do, and not be energized or empowered by it. So believe in those hidden spiritual forces residing within you, and humbly but consciously release them to flow outward from you to touch those with whom you pray, along with the checkout clerk, a troubled-looking street person, and all those you encounter. Become a walking, human, holy dynamo.

Secular saints like you are changing the church, not by changing the institution, but more importantly by affecting the body of Christ—making it holier and richer in spirit. Blessedly you and countless others are actively doing this, and the effects of your influence on the body of Christ are far beyond your realization. As old veterans of the Second Vatican Council reforms of the 1960s, we both dream of a day when that springtime of renewal we found so full of life will reappear. You, Joe, are that springtime of faith! Each time your personal prayer is incarnated into your communal worship, that divine spring draws closer.

One final suggestion is to use your friendship with your pastor as a doorway to speak to him, gently encouraging him to include subjects in his homilies that touch upon the daily lives and real struggles of his people. But more important than that, when you are in church, even when seated way back in a pew, consciously send waves of your spiritual energy up to the pulpit, wrapping your pastor in light. You can consciously spin webs of light outward from you to encircle those who are present and worshipping with you. As you perform these spiritual exercises, be aware that these webs of divine light you see only in your imagination truly exist if you but passionately desire to transmit them forth from your heart.

Prayer and friendship are beyond the restraints of space and time, so I ask in closing that you send this old friend some of that energy you generate in your prayers. Blessings on you and Betty, and also on your decisions about your relationship with God and the church.

Letter to Joanne
Affirming Her Church Attendance

Dear Joanne,

This letter is in response to yours in which you wrote of your growing sense that perhaps it is time for you to stop attending Sunday services. Those who have decided to exit the institutional Church could be called "Exodus Christians," but you wrote that such a decision was troubling for you since you have practiced your faith your entire lifetime. Well, Joanne, do you recall the old saying, "Practice makes perfect"?

I write to encourage you to practice your faith by doing something different when you go to church. I propose you practice going to church as you did years and years ago, before, like the rest of us, you became a convert to consumerism! Allow me to explain. The author of several excellent books on religion, Karen Armstrong, makes an intriguing observation when she says that religion for many people today has become just another consumer item or service. This concept of religion as just another commodity asks these questions: "How many people practice (that is *use*) their religion to undergo a life transformation?" and "How many go to church not to be changed at all but simply to obtain a weekly emotional or spiritual uplift?"

Religion, as part of society, can't escape being swept up into the magnetic whirlpool of consumerism that so dominates our culture. Your parish church or any church today, by providing a spiritual service, can easily be like a Wal-Mart or Taco Bell. Churches, like chain restaurants or businesses, are also eager to attract customers. I realize referring to parishioners as customers is shocking, if not scandalous. But in our culture, influenced profoundly by consumerism, many churchgoers approach

religious services as just another service or product they ac-
quire. As a result of this consumer attitude, they go to church
expecting good service, good music, and stimulating yet com-
fortable sermons (meaning those that don't disturb their bias-
es, prejudices, or social practices). Instead of approaching their
pastor with a sense of reverence traditionally shown to spiritual
leaders, they tend to regard him or her as the general manager
of their local religious franchise, and so complain when they
feel "the service" wasn't good. Customers expect and demand
good service, and the wealthier they are, the better service they
demand.

Whenever customer-Christians find the religious service
or the reverend local franchise manager unpleasant or disap-
pointing, they simply "go" elsewhere on Sunday—to another
church, to the golf course, or out for a leisurely Sunday bunch.
This preface about religious consumerism is important since it
can be one explanation of today's attitude about church attendance. Now I will return to my proposal about "practicing the
faith" as you did many, many years ago.

As an American Christian you have always practiced your
faith while living in a secular culture. In a secular society,
churches are sacred zones or places set aside for God encounters. Regardless of the sermons and the quality of the music (or
lack of it), the physical church structure provides you a quiet
setting for a personal, prayerful encounter with the sacred in an
otherwise secular cityscape. If you desire to return to "practicing" that former expression of your faith, consider giving a deaf
ear to sermons that continuously harp on certain moral themes
or attempt to instruct you on how to vote. Being deaf to what
your ears find offensive, your soul can absorb the Presence of
God and drift off into prayer. The presence of those there in

church worshiping with you is a tangible sign of the faith community to which you belong, and they remind you that the way to God is a collective one, in which each of us goes to God together with the rest of the Body of Christ.

So I encourage you to strive to remain faithful in your church attendance by hanging on to the hope of the perennial rotation of pastors. Some day in the near future you may get a new pastor, God willing, who will create enriching, good liturgies that will inspire you and others. Meanwhile, more than simply practicing your faith, you must strive to deepen it.

Your home can, and should be, a domestic church where you worship God daily by prayer, reflection, and ritual. However, remember the influence of your personal religious history, in which you have consciously sought the presence of the holy and found it easier to pray in the sacred space of a church. Since childhood, sacred architecture and art has had a powerful unconscious influence upon all of our spiritual lives and us. So instead of considering the once-a-week Sunday obligation as a requirement that you must fulfill in church, look upon it as a "Sunday opportunity." View it as a weekly opportunity to be spiritually inspired, to be moved to prayer, and to experience serenity by being in a house of prayer.

I would suggest using this opportunity to the fullest: "Go early and stay late!" Remain in church quietly praying after everyone else has departed. Use the times before and after the communal worship for your personal prayer, or just sit peacefully. Allow your soul to absorb the graces flowing out of the powerful sacred environment. As the body finds life-sustaining benefits by simply breathing outside in the clear fresh air, so likewise the soul is nourished by quietly spending time in a truly sacred place. While nothing may change in the parish liturgies or the content of the homilies, I assure you, Joanne, that you will be changed by your weekly times of prayerful silence!

Life is a process of growth, and the same is true of your soul and faith. I invite you, along with adding this contemplative time in church and attending weekly communal worship, to ask yourself what personal spiritual needs are not met by going to church. These needs could include instruction in prayer and meditation, and perhaps a need for spiritual direction, since these are not resources provided by the typical parish church. So go looking to fill these needs elsewhere, such as at a bookstore. Spiritual books make excellent guides for prayer, even for spiritual direction. Reading scripture is beneficial, especially with a study guide. Regardless of what you seek, remember the old adage, "When the student is ready, the teacher will appear!"

If you truly desire to grow a large soul and seek a spiritual coach who will lead you to holiness, then consider a thoughtful reading of the instructions Jesus gave to his disciples in chapters 5–7 of Matthew's Gospel. These pages contain the heroic call to holiness that I feel you seek. So read, and reread, and then read them again, committing them to memory. They will be your spiritual coach, challenging you to grow in holiness and in the image of Jesus.

Finally, returning to your prayer times before and after the parish worship, I encourage you to pray for your pastor. Petition the Holy Spirit to inspire him to become not simply a competent administrator, but a true spiritual leader more concerned about the prayer life of his people than the raising of money. Pray that he becomes a compassionate shepherd who feeds his sheep with well-prepared homilies. Pray he will guide them in how to live out the gospel and how to become holy in the midst of their lives in the world.

Again, thank you for your letter. It is my prayerful hope that you will find a personal renewal of spirit by your new approach to your Sunday "opportunities."

Letter to Larry
About the Critical Need of Continuing to Have Hope in Religious Evolution

Dear Larry,

In our last conversation you again repeated to me your favorite quote from the *Pastoral Constitution on the Church in the Modern World* of the Second Vatican Council, which speaks to an important need of the church "to scrutinize the signs of the times and interpret them in the light of the gospel." You said that today the signs are thunderously loud, not only here in this country but in Europe and elsewhere, as countless millions of believers have stopped attending church. In North America the number of non-attending is now 70 percent, and in Europe, as high as 85 percent, and in that traditionally Catholic country of Austria it is 90 percent! Such a massive historical exodus is unmistakably a "sign of the times," yet the institutional Catholic Church, instead of scrutinizing this historic exodus and interpreting it as a need for radical changes, condemns those who have stopped going to church as being weak in their faith and seduced by the lax and hedonistic Western culture.

You've asked rhetorically, "Tell me, why should I stay involved in the Church and continue attending my parish?" You've shared with me before that your wife is so disgruntled with the lack of inspiration and the poor quality of worship that she has for years now no longer accompanied you to Mass. So I can understand that you have grown disheartened yourself. As you said, at least in a democracy you have hope. If the present political administration is deceitful, corrupt, and incompetent, you always have the hope at the next election that people will vote in a new government. However, with the Church there's no such hope for any change in the near future upon which to cling! So you say, "For those countless others like me, who are despondent, doubtful that anything will ever change, why not just quietly fade away? In fact, I'll bet if I did just that, no one at church would even notice my absence."

Sadly, I empathize with your hopelessness, but I have a proposal that is a slight twist on your favorite quote from the Vatican Council. My proposal is "We, the church, need to interpret these hopeless signs of the times in the light of evolution"—making the one word change of "evolution" for "gospel." In the early sixties, the Vatican Council created perhaps the greatest innovation in church history. It filled you and me, as well as millions of others, with great enthusiasm and hope about our faith that we felt sure was but the beginning of further changes that were unfolding. Some called that Vatican Council, which also inspired those in mainline churches, a revolution, but more correctly it was an evolutionary event. If we had properly named that spirit event of the 1960s and also had understood the nature of evolution, then we would not be surprised at the regrettable reversals by the Church in these past several years.

New research in human evolution shows that our species evolved by fits and starts. Our human evolution, says the paleontologist Ian Tattersall, was one of amazing beginnings and growth, then long periods where nothing happened, punctuated by eruptions of fantastic change. Now take this description of the process of evolution and compare it to the Church. It was static, largely unchanging for hundreds of years, even as the world in which it existed was dramatically changing. Then in middle of the twentieth century occurred the sudden, unexpected "eruption" of the Second Vatican Council with its wondrous renewal agenda to involve the Church in the modern world. That evolutionary upsurge of new life changed forever so many of us who were gifted to be part of it. After that charismatic burst of dynamic energy of change, we are now living in one of those "long periods where nothing happens," and in which there is actually a regression.

It is critical to acknowledge that the liturgical changes designed to return us to the practice of the early church and the scriptural renewal of Vatican II did not appear out of thin air. Scholars had been writing about and proposing reforms for decades before the Council. As a result, the Church could be said to have been pregnant with these dreams and scholarly insights that were birthed into the documents of that council.

So, Larry, you are like those who seeded the Church at the end of the nineteenth and the beginning of the twentieth centuries by their scholarship and dreams of returning to a closer resemblance of the apostolic Church. Both publicly and in your parish discussion group you have advocated the ordination of women, a married clergy, optional celibacy, and lay administration of local Christian communities, along with intercommunion and interchange with other Christian churches. You and others are seeding the soil for the next "eruption" of the Spirit. If you just fade away, drop out and leave the Church, you could perhaps take with you these dynamic seeds of what I feel will be an even greater eruption of the Spirit of God than the one we witnessed in the Second Vatican Council. Dreaming is evolutionary seeding, and the envisioning of a sacred future event requires dedication and sacrifice—that of not living to see this next major evolutionary event!

As I conclude this letter, I again encourage you, regardless of how difficult it seems at times, to remain as committed as you can to the Church. While likely you will never see the harvest of your efforts, this possibility shouldn't diminish your commitment. For as that old favorite saying of mine goes, "Any dream that can be realized in your lifetime isn't worth giving your life for!"

Letter to Patricia
About Faith and the Christian Life

Dear Patricia,

At our lunch the other day, Patricia, just as we were concluding, you asked me when people know if they have lost their faith or if it has grown to the point where they are no longer religious in the common understanding of being religious. I joked that such an involved question deserved more than a few parting words, and as we parted, I promised to write this letter.

Your insight about faith as a growing reality is valid, since faith typically advances through various degrees or stages. It is also possible to incorrectly diagnose a matured faith as being a lost one. You've heard the old expression "Keep the faith," which isn't the same as "Keep your hat on," since faith isn't some unchanging thing like one's hat. Religious faith undergoes gradual changes at various ages or stages in life, or it can dynamically change at some pivotal life moment. A person's faith can—as a result of some major life trauma, disaster, or serious sickness—increase or decrease.

Religious faith can mean a belief in the teachings of one's religion or in the existence of God, along with other spiritual beliefs. In the New Testament, faith is called a gift. This implies that some are more gifted than others with belief, and also that some are not given the gift. Like natural talents or gifts— intellectual, athletic, musical, or artistic—the gift of faith also apparently is given in varying degrees to various people.

You asked, Patricia, if a person who had developed a mature faith needed to continue to attend church. First, that is an excellent question, since ceasing to be engaged in communal worship can have significant consequences. So before you decide to no longer engage in attending church, I encourage you to examine the degree of your personal faith at this time in your life. To assist you in this self-faith test, I offer the following levels of faith belief.

1. The faith of a **preschool child** is that of a primitive being, undefined and tending to be connected to powerful figures like the child's parents. Understandably, this linking of God with parents can have an impact on one's relationship with God later in life. This can be especially harmful if the parental relationship isn't a good one. Parental names for God, such as Father or Mother, carry with them a lot of childhood baggage—sometimes good, sometimes not.

2. In **middle childhood**, faith acquires a sense of certainty and is very literal. However, religious language by necessity is symbolic, so childhood faith must by necessity move beyond dependency on what is factually true.

3. As faith evolves into **adolescent faith**, it becomes a belief that is unexamined and typically conforms to the beliefs of friends or parents. Adolescence is a time to rebel as a sign of self-determination, so adolescents can rebel against religion as a type of teenage agnosticism. Paradoxically, adolescent faith can also be a very religious time, often accompanied by aspirations to high spiritual goals or religious vocations. It is typically a stage when the adolescent is very critical of hypocrisy. Studies show that in life there are two peak times of religious fervor: adolescence and the mid-life forties. The recorded lives of holy people often show these faith periods to be the times of their religious conversion or inspiration.

4. In **early adulthood**, faith changes in both belief and practice as young adults evolve their own values instead of continuing to practice those they inherited from their parents.

5. The faith stage is that of **mature adulthood,** which can be a mixture of skepticism and routine religious practice often promoted by being a parent. Children require being accompanied to worship, and so the parent routinely attends church, even if he or she personally would not if it were not for the sake of their children. For some, faith now can reach back to embrace certain religious practices discarded in earlier ages.

6. In **late adulthood**, faith, depending upon the individual, can bloom and open up like the blossom of a flower and be cross-fertilized by spiritual insights from other world religions. For others in late adulthood, faith can fossilize as they seek dogmatic security in the midst of rapid changes in society and in their bodies' aging. Typically, adults, having reached one of these latter stages in faith, can remain there for a lifetime. Along with these, there is another category of those who could be said to have a "pious" faith. While they are mature adults, they have a childlike faith. It is one of literal certainty about religious matters, a fascination with the miraculous, and unquestioned obedience to and acceptance of the teachings of their religion.

7. There remains yet another degree or stage of faith, the **serene faith of intimate unity with the Divine Mystery**. Those at this faith level could be called faithless, and by that I mean they no longer believe, they know! Their

knowing isn't the same as childhood literal certainty; rather, it is a trusting acceptance without evidence or proof in the Divine Mystery as a holy inscrutability. On the surface this stage of faith can appear as agnostic, but in reality it is that of a lover's unconditional trust in the beloved. Those who, like a flower, have organically evolved to this degree of faith may no longer feel the need for institutional religion, yet on occasions they continue to be involved in religious rituals and worship.

Some believe that only a rare few ever reach this seventh level of belief. That may be true, but it is also possible that those who believe this way either underestimate the growth capacity of the gift of faith or—since they have not experienced it themselves—doubt that many can reach it. So the question, Patricia, is: "Have you, by your openness to spiritual growth, evolved to a point where you haven't lost your faith, but simply no longer have need of its religious constructs?" Trust, another name for faith, grows with love, and the more you love, the more you trust, until you reach a level of an unconditional, unquestioned trust. The great commandment isn't to attend Sunday worship, but to love God with all your heart, soul, mind, and body. Our love of God is expressed not in flights of ecstasy, but in loving others, in deeds of caring for the needy and neglected, and loving acceptance of those who are different than you.

In concluding, let us return to the faith stages in your life. Since belief is such a nebulous reality, don't be concerned if you can't pinpoint at this moment your stage of faith. You could actually be at a personal, unique combination of several stages or in the midst of undergoing a faith transition. I also realize attempts to clarify a situation often can cause more confusion than was originally the case, so if this is your situation, please write and I will respond as best I can.

Meanwhile, I encourage you to continue to be faithful to your meditational prayer life and reading. I close with a prayerful hope that you experience a sense of tranquility in your relentless religious search, and instead of closing with the old blessing "Keep the faith," my wish for you, Patricia, is "Keep growing your faith."

fOUR

Letters to the Anointed Members of the priesthood of the Baptized

The following letters deal with how Christians can respond when the ordained clergy cannot, or will not, perform for them religious rituals like weddings, baptisms, burials, and other rites of the faithful. Their reasons may include an invalid marriage on the part of one or both of those requesting marriage, even if the couple faithfully attends Sunday worship. The inability to have a church wedding or burial may also be denied if those requesting them are judged as non-practicing, meaning non-church attending. So as Exodus Christians, after having made every effort to have a ceremony performed in a church and unable to find an ordained minister to do so, what options do you have for celebrating your wedding, having your baby baptized, or celebrating a Christian funeral?

Since the heart of the heritage that Jesus of Nazareth left to his disciples is his memorial Last Supper Meal, that ancient and central ritual of the faithful will also be explored in this chapter for what is possible without an ordained minister. It is most important that the proposals in the following letters be seen only as a last resort after every other attempt has been met with rejection or failure. Christians of mainline churches of course prefer an ordained minister, as they have grown up in a culture where their clergy performed the sacred rites that mark the great passages of life and death.

While today a very clear and theological difference is made between the baptized faithful and the baptized ordained faithful, this was not always the case in Christianity. From the gospels it is clear that Jesus himself established no priesthood or clergy and made no distinctions in rank between his baptized disciples. After his death, this attitude continued in the earliest days of the infant, post-resurrection church.

These early churches were small in number, but any group over eight or ten needs a leader, and if no one officially occupies this role then some member of the group will always assume that position. In the early Christian communities, the host or hostess was logically the leader of the community and presided over the ritual celebrations conducted at that house church. As the number of Christians grew, so did the need for leaders of larger groups, and so the early Christians borrowed from their Jewish ancestry the tradition of choosing an elder or elders to lead their common prayer.

Within fifty to seventy years the office of elders arose and eventually evolved into today's ordained clergy. While Christian clergy presided at liturgical rituals of the Lord's Supper and other blessings, they were not required for Christian marriage and burial for almost another nine hundred to a thousand years.

The letters in this chapter address how today's Exodus Christians might return to Christianity's earliest roots and mark the great passages of life and death as faithful followers of Christ, even when they are no longer able to go to church.

A Letter About Celebrating Christian Marriage in the Absence of a Parish Church or an Ordained Minister

Dear Comrades in Christ,

Marriage invokes memories and images of a beautiful bride in a long white dress and a formally attired groom encircled by flowers standing at an altar before a robed minister. Not only have religious tradition or laws created this image, motion pictures and television have etched our consciousness with this image of fairytale weddings in church. There's nothing romantic about being married in a drab office at city hall, with some anonymous clerk officiating. It is no wonder that Christians, even those who no longer attend church, desire a religious ceremony and a church for this most significant event in their lives.

Yet after having attempted to be married in your own parish or church, only to be met by frustration and rejection, what other options are possible for a Christian couple in love and ready to publicly commit their lives to one another? The second most frequently chosen option is to have your marriage in another Christian church rather than your own. The pastor, being an ordained minister of God, can witness your vows before God, who blesses and binds you as husband and wife regardless of who is standing in front of you. After failing to be able to be married in your church, this last resort resolution can for some create problems with parents and family who are religious. But I assure you it will create no problems with God! In John's Gospel (14: 2) Jesus tells us, "In my Father's house there are many dwelling places." If Jesus was among us today, he would surely add, "And what is true in heaven, is equally true here on earth!"

To be married outside of your religious tradition in another church because you can't find an ordained minister in your own to perform the ceremony can be the source of pain to the parents of either the groom or bride, or both. It would only be natural to try to avoid this pain, but I encourage those who must confront this dilemma of parental objection to trust and love. It takes two sides to create a lasting division, so regardless of their negative response, if you continue to bridge that chasm with love, in time the wound will heal. And there is another important reason to follow your heart and your conscience in pursuing an action opposed by your parents.

Allow me to relate a personal story. Back in 1920, my own Catholic father fell in love with a Protestant woman, my mother, who was a devoted member of the Disciples of Christ Church. His Irish Catholic family was greatly distressed and opposed to their "mixed" marriage; they wanted him to marry a Catholic. My mother's Protestant family was even more strongly opposed to the wedding. My mother told me that, upon hearing the news of marriage, her grandmother said she would rather see her granddaughter dead than marry a Catholic!

My dad and mom, being very much in love, weathered the objections and opposition of their families and were finally married. Their wedding, however, wasn't that much different than the civil service in a courthouse. They were married in front of a black-suited priest in the drab parish office at the rectory of my father's parish church, no doubt with a large photo of stern-faced Pope Benedict XV looking down on them. Because my mother was a Protestant, they were not permitted a traditional beautiful wedding inside a Catholic church! No flowing white bridal attire for my mom; there was no wedding music or flowers, just an office desk, a couple of chairs, and drab gray filing cabinets. Paradoxically, after such a rebuff from the church, she became a Catholic five years later, and remained a prayerful and faithful one for her entire life.

This painful experience of my parents' wedding has been for me an important life lesson. From it I learned that regardless of the emotional pain and trauma, it is necessary to leave home if you are truly to have your own life. We usually leave home in stages, and sadly many never completely leave. As adults, they continue to be dominated by the decisions and wishes of their parents. As a result, the critical decision about the person whom you choose to love and then marry, and where your wedding will take place, can be a healthy and good separation from one's parents. I say "good" since such a parental home leaving can give birth to a healthy, mature parent-adult son or daughter relationship. But, as I suggest risking parental displeasure, in no way do I want to diminish the pain that such a severance can cause, and I understand why it can be so undesirable.

So after having met with rejection from their own church, what options does a Christian couple have when they want to be married? The problem presents a wonderful occasion to experience a key element in successful married love: compromise. The couple must explore the options and find one that will as best as possible meet each of their personal religious and emotional needs. Here for your consideration are a few options.

1. If you are a Catholic, consider having your wedding ceremony in a Protestant church; if you are a Protestant then consider some non-denominational church.

2. Consider a non-church site such as a hotel or reception hall, and be married in a service conducted by a minister of some other religious affiliation.

3. Choose an Eden wedding in some beautiful outdoor location that echoes the very first of all marriages held in the midst of creation with God officiating. This optional wedding ceremony can be conducted by a lay friend, but for it to be a legal marriage you are also required to have a civil marriage service.

4. Be married in a brief, civil ceremony at city hall, where God blesses and joins you in marriage as your wedding vows are witnessed by a civil authority for legal purposes. After this civil marriage, you can have a beautiful wedding reception celebration with your friends, and those of the family who would like to be present can be. At this post-civil marriage reception, you can recite again your marriage vows and then ask those present to bless both of you and your marriage. It will be beautiful if at this repeated exchange of vows and rings, your parents can bestow upon the two of you their parental blessing, as once did the patriarchs and matriarchs of biblical and even apostolic families.

For Christians unable to have an ordained cleric witness their vows and officiate at their wedding, creating their own wedding ceremony with family and friends is but a return to a twelve hundred year tradition of Christianity. In the early centuries of Christianity, marriage was a family and secular event, with the bride's father playing the chief role in the wedding ceremony. Relics of this remain in our contemporary marriage ceremonies where the father of the bride escorts her to the altar. Late in the fourth century, a custom developed in some places for the bishop or a priest to bless the newly wedded couple either before the wedding or at the wedding reception. Over the next two centuries, the clergy gradually began to play a more active role in marriage rituals by acts like joining the couple's hands together or saying a blessing over them. In the fourth century, marriages solemnized by a priest were only mandatory for marriages of priests and clerics, and by the eighth century this requirement was expanded to include the nobility. By the seventh century it still wasn't mandatory that a priest be present at the marriage of other Christians. Even by the year AD 1000 there was not yet an obligatory church ritual ceremony for marriages. However, by the twelfth century, laws were established requiring a church wedding ceremony conducted exclusively by an ordained cleric. Several centuries later, the requirement that a couple be married in church and by a priest became absolute. A failure to be married in this way resulted in the marriage not being recognized by the Church, and thus the bridal couple was barred from receiving Holy Communion and the other sacraments.

For many in recent decades, the desire for a church wedding with all the elaborate trimmings is not so much to conform to a Church law or even the desire to be married in Christ. For many the church structure (especially a Gothic church with a long aisle for the bridal procession), organ music, and a presiding ordained minister is little more than an essential backdrop for today's concept of a "beautiful" wedding.

This abridged history of church rituals of marriage is important for Exodus Christians to remember. The obligation to be married by an ordained minister, which we sometimes think of as an ancient practice, has only been mandatory for the entire church since the twelfth century! In the two thousand year history of Christianity, that is a relatively recent custom.

A Prayer Before Marriage in A Church Not Your Own

O God, you know we were denied
when we asked to be married in our own church.
We are grateful that another Christian church
has welcomed us and that their minister
will witness our marriage in Christ.
While we are disappointed, we proclaim, O God,
that you dwell in all places of prayer.

O God of Love, you who have witnessed
all marriages since the beginning of time,
be present at the church of our wedding.
There, with you and all your holy saints,
we will pledge our love and lives as one for life.

May all our family's holy ancestors now at rest among
   your saints
be present to witness and bless our marriage to one
   another.
United in God, they'll not be disturbed by the church
   in which we are married,
since they see not minor faith differences,
but rather the unity of all Christian churches.

May these our saintly wedding guests
whisper their heavenly wisdom into the ears
of our family members and friends who gather with
   us on this day.
May all feel at home, and in church, at our wedding
   and in our married life.
Amen.

A Prayer at Home Before or After a Civil Marriage Ceremony

O Lord, you who joined Adam and Eve as one,
we regret that circumstances prevent a church
   wedding for us
where you would richly bless our marriage.
We pause to pray before we depart for a civil
   ceremony
that will bind us together legally as husband and wife.
or
[We pause to pray following our civil wedding
   ceremony that has joined us together legally as
   husband and wife.]

What we truly desire is a sacred binding together
that only you who are Love Eternal can grant us.
We acknowledge that you dwell in all places,
and so are present in the love between the two of us.
Therefore, before you, Our God, we profess our vows.

The two join their right hands and the groom begins:

I, _____, take you, _____,
to be my wife, and I pledge before God
to be faithful to you
in good times and in bad, in sickness and in health,
until death do us part.

The bride then continues:

I, _____, take you, _____,
to be my husband, and I pledge before God
to be faithful to you

in good times and in bad, in sickness and in health,
until death do us part.

Pour forth, O Lord God,
the fullness of your blessings upon the two of us
whose vows of love until death you have witnessed
and whom you unite together in marriage this day.

*The exchange of wedding rings is repeated by both bride
and groom.*

This wedding ring is an unbroken sign
of my fidelity and love for you;
may it remind you always of our sacred
covenant that God has witnessed today.

A nuptial kiss is exchanged.

Concluding Prayer I
This is prayed before going for a civil ceremony.

Come, our Beloved God, and escort us now as we
    depart
to perform the required civil ceremony required by
    state law.

Concluding Prayer II
*This is used if the ritual has taken place after having a civil marriage
ceremony.*

Either bride or groom prays aloud:
Dear friends,

_____ and I thank you for your presence with
    us today,
here at our simple home wedding.
Grateful for your understanding and support,

we conclude this wedding celebration by daring to
   ask of you another gift.
As we bow our heads, please raise your hands over us
and silently call down God's nuptial blessing upon us
as husband and wife.

*Silent blessing prayer or invite guests to pray (or sing) a
   blessing aloud.*

At the conclusion:
May God enrich all of us with love,
and with a long and good life.
Amen.

An Exodus Letter About Infant Baptism

Dear Companions in Christ,

As Exodus Christians and parents of a newly born child, you desired to have him baptized, but when you approached the local parish pastor, he refused. You honestly answered his questions about your Sunday attendance, saying that you did attend on Christmas, Easter, and special occasions, but you did not attend as regular practice. The pastor said your failure to attend church on a regular basis disqualified you from having your baby baptized. Since you refused to pledge to do this as a requirement for him to baptize your child, you thanked him and left. Now you feel pressure from your parents to have your child baptized and wonder what you should do.

Allow me to offer some pastoral advice by asking some questions. Is the baptism of your son truly your desire or is it a need of your church-attending parents or grandparents? If without outside pressure you desire this, may I ask why, other than tradition, you desire that your baby be baptized as a Christian? Note, I said "Christian" since baptism does not baptize one into the Catholic, Baptist, Episcopal or any church, but rather into Christ. So do you desire that your child becomes a Christian?

Even if you do not regularly attend weekly worship, do you consider yourselves to be Christians? Do you believe that you practice the teachings of Jesus to the best of your ability, striving to address the needs of the poor and needy? Baptism isn't magical! While one is baptized into the risen Christ, that person must grow into being a Christian by being educating about the faith and practicing its traditions and ways of living. This being so, the most important question is whether the two of you are willing to make years of effort instructing your son in the teachings of Jesus and living a good Christian life. This formation in religious values and practices requires teaching your son by example and not by simply sending him for religious education. The old rule of thumb was that the mother teaches religious values and the father teaches religious practice. But it takes consistent commitment on the part of both of you to raise a Christian.

Baptizing an infant is not like vaccinating your child against disease. Baptism requires a mature decision to undergo a life transformation and become a follower of Jesus Christ or—in the case of parents seeking baptism for a child—assuming the responsibility of handing on the faith to one's child. In early Christianity baptism was typically an adult ritual. Infant baptisms began when parents desired that their children be baptized along with them, so that their entire family would be Christian. This parental aspiration changed from an ideal to a need in the fourth century, with the introduction of the idea of original sin being inherited from Adam, creating in an infant a condition spoken of as "contagion of death." Baptizing a child thus was required to restore the child to God's grace both now and in the life to come.

Today, theologians more commonly view original sin as the universal condition of all human life and society. It is a common state into which we are born where evil restricts our freedom rather than it being seen as some ancient sin-stain biologically transmitted from generation to generation. Today the baptism of a newborn infant offers the opportunity for the parents to celebrate with family and friends the gift of life they have been given and to ask the community of faith to welcome their child. This water ritual is also a second birth into the mystery of Christ's Body by which the child is proclaimed to now belong to larger family, the Christian family and indeed to all of

God's cosmos rather than to only the limited family of his birth parents. Finally, the baptismal ritual also provides a public opportunity for parents, godparents, and the entire community to express gratitude to the Divine Parent for the gift of this child, whose very presence speaks to them of the presence of God.

Before we conclude, let's return to the beginning of this Exodus letter, where the pastor told the non-church attending parents that he would baptize their child only if they pledged to return to weekly attendance at church and to more fully practice their faith. While you originally rejected this offer, consider it again now but do so thoughtfully and thoroughly. By raising your son as a member of a church and as a Christian, you give him a religious tradition, the richest of inheritances since it provides spiritual roots. When he reaches young adulthood, he will choose on his own to continue to be or not to be a member of a church, and even if he will be Christian. I asked you to thoroughly examine baptizing your child, since by agreeing to raise him in a religious home, you are committing yourself to eighteen or so years of living your religious faith and teaching him by example and education how to be a faithful Christian. Painstakingly examine such a commitment.

Under ordinary circumstances it would be the pastor or an ordained minister of the Church who would baptize your child. Since early times, the continuous theology of the Church has been that since Jesus made baptism essential to Christian life, in exceptional circumstances any baptized Christian can baptize. So if after reflecting on these questions I have raised, you still desire to welcome your baby with a ceremony, reclaim the practice of those early catacomb Christians and welcome your baby yourselves with a home celebration and ritual blessing. While the institutional church may not formally recognize yours as an

extreme enough circumstance to warrant you baptizing your
baby, a homegrown ritual celebration may help you mark the
birth of your child with holy welcome and make formal (and
perhaps public) your commitment to raising your child as a
Christian.

Blessing of Holy Water

*The use of holy water in ritual sprinkling or immersion is a Christian
tradition that has long been used not only at church for celebrations of
baptism, weddings, funerals and the like, but also in many Christian
homes. Among other things, Christian households can use holy water to mark family members with the sign of the cross on entering or
leaving the home; as part of children's nighttime prayer; and for the
blessing of holiday tables, Christmas trees, and Easter foods. Water
symbolizes cleansing, sanctification and the descent of God's graces.
Any Christian can bless water by asking God to be present in it and
through it.*

*After welcoming any family members and friends who have gath-
ered, the mother, father or another adult prayer leader should call the
group to gather around a vessel of warm water.*

After a moment of silent stillness:
Good and loving God,
we call upon your power today as we bless this water.
All water is holy, for before the earth was formed
you sent your Spirit sweeping as a mighty wind
over the waters that covered all of our planet.

While slowly making the sign of the cross over the water:
Send forth your Holy Spirit now into this water
to impregnate it with your invigorating grace.
May your creative, protecting presence be
wherever this holy water is used.

May its life-giving power strengthen and renew us.
Amen.

Prayer and Ritual Blessing to Welcome a Child

*The mother, father, or other appropriate person holds the infant.
Addressing the infant, one of the parents says:*

We believe that William Wordsworth spoke
accurately of you _____when he said,
"Trailing clouds of glory do we come from God, who
is our home:
Heaven lies about us in our infancy."

We believe, dear child, that not in shame or sin but in
glory
have you come to us from God.
We know that heaven is about us here in your
presence
and our hearts overflow with joy and gratitude.

With hands uplifted in prayer:

God, whom we call Father, and who mothers us
with unconditional love and tender care,
come to our aid in what we are about to do.
Conditions prevent us from baptizing our child
as our parents took us to church to be baptized.

Central to baptism is the act of naming one in Christ,
and so we ask you, our God, to grace us as today
as we name our child _____
and claim her/him as a child of God and follower of
Christ.

We bless our child with the Sign of the Cross.

Parents dip their hand into the blessed water and trace the cross on the infant's head or make the sign of the cross in the usual manner by touching head, chest, and shoulders saying:

By this holy Sign of the Cross
may _____ be forever one with
   Christ,
and so be shielded from all severe harm,
deadly disease, and from all evil.

As parents and all others present bless themselves with the water in the Sign of the Cross:

May our good and gracious God, bless and keep us all,
guide us and mold us as true disciples,
and protect us all our days.
Amen.

A Letter on Care
of the Dying for Exodus Christians

Dear Companions in Christ,

The sacrament of anointing with holy oil is a significant part of dying for Christians, especially those of the Roman Catholic tradition. It cannot be overlooked in the pastoral care of Exodus Christians. When this anointing is given to those who are dying, it is a sacred action of assisting them in their departure from this world. It provides spiritual comfort and reassurance as they begin the last and most significant transition of their lives. An ordained priest is the minister of the anointing of the dying, and rare would be the priest who would not give this sacrament to a dying person, even if they had not been inside a church for many years.

Personally, I have known people who, after some previous painful encounter with the Church or some of its clergy, have left never to return. As a result of this unfortunate experience of rejection they do not want a priest to come to them on their deathbed to anoint them. Perhaps one reason is that part of the anointing ritual is the confession of sins to the priest. This implies a penitential return to a church they have no desire to embrace. Frequently, however, the dying person who is still a Christian and who has never stopped considering himself or herself Catholic, desires some kind of final religious ritual of the dying. Often this is not only the religious desire of the dying person but also that of his or her family.

Before I make a proposal for addressing the spiritual needs of an Exodus Christian who is dying and the special needs of their family, a brief reflection on the ancient tradition of the anointing of the sick and the dying might be helpful.

In the ancient world, sickness and sin were intertwined, as is clear from the healings of Jesus in the Gospels. Lacking any knowledge of germs and viruses, diseases were believed to be caused by demons or were viewed as divine punishments for personal sin and even the sins of one's parents. This ancient connection between sin and sickness explains the inclusion of confession and absolution that today is part of the anointing ritual. References found in the New Testament give evidence that in the apostolic church the elders anointed the sick with oil and surrounded them with prayer. While references to anointing with oil in the next century are scarce, it is obvious that it continued in some form because of a text found in the *Apostolic Tradition* of the year 215 that contained a blessing prayer for oil. In the ancient world olive oil was used for medicinal purposes, and early Christians considered blessed oil to be an extremely helpful remedy. The bishop prayed over the oil "may it give strength to all who taste it and strength to all who use it." Then the faithful took that blessed oil home to be used as medicine for body and soul.

When Exodus Christians must respond to the wishes of a dying parent or spouse who does not desire reconciliation with the institutional Church, the following words of a fifth century pope can be helpful. In 416, Pope Innocent I wrote in a letter to the bishop of Gubbio, "Not only priests, but all Christians may use this oil for anointing, when either they or members of their household have need of it." In the sixth century, this practice of the laity anointing the sick and dying was the common custom in parts of France. Caesarius of Arles, like Pope Innocent, urged his people in sermons to use blessed oils for anointing the sick. He said they would receive health of body and pardon of sins by the anointing.

While later centuries restricted the anointing of the sick to priests only (which continues to this day), this institutional practice does not negate the words of Pope Innocent I. If baptism is being incorporated into the fullness of Christ, then every baptized person is invested with the powers or graces to act, as did Jesus Christ, in order to respond to the needs he or she encounters in the world of today. While by law and tradition the ordained clergy are the official ministers of these sacred rituals of life and death, is our excessively generous and loving God thereby restricted from using other human instruments as channels of grace, healing reconciliation, and peace?

Prayer for a Dying Exodus Christian

O Compassionate and loving God,
hear our prayers for _____,
who is taking his/her last steps through the door of
    death
to go home to you.
Sacred is this hour of death,
and holy is this place where this world and the next
join hands as one in time.

As you know, we now are without a pastor,
other than you who have guided us faithfully through
    many struggles.
Come now, Pastor of Pastors.
May your presence wipe away the frightening fears of
    death.
Caress _____ gently with your goodness
to awaken in him/her a steadfast hope in the life
that awaits him/her on other side of death's door.

Our dear _____,
we now release you to leave us
and we place you into God's hands.
Go now with God and with all the saints;
go in peace through death to life without end.
Amen

A simple anointing of the dying person with fragrant oil might follow the prayer.

A Letter on Funeral Services for Exodus Christians in the Absence of a Parish Church or Ordained Minister

Dear Companions in Christ,

After marriage, the second and even more important time Exodus Christians are confronted with the need for religion and for church membership is at the time of death of a spouse, life companion, or family member. If the deceased or the family requesting their burial does not belong to a parish or if the deceased did not faithfully attend church and over the years contribute financially to the parish, the pastor sometimes refuses to preside at the funeral. This strict limitation of who can and who cannot be buried from the church is especially true in certain dioceses or sections of the country and in parishes where the pastor is rigidly authoritarian.

Since no one wants the undertaker to bury a spouse or mother, the search begins to find a minister of some church who will perform this last religious act. Typically non-denominational ministers are more open than the clergy of mainline churches to performing both marriages and funerals. Usually funeral directors know of clergy who are available for such non-church funerals. Whatever minister is found will typically not have known the deceased, but will conduct a religious funeral service in the mortuary chapel and preside at the cemetery interment. Depending upon where you live, some clergy of your own faith will conduct religious services at funeral homes and even perform the burials rites of those who, for one reason or another, cannot have or do not wish to have an in-church service.

Historically, church funeral rituals did not appear for hundreds of years, and for early Christians, funerals were like

marriages—family religion affairs. The family would wash
the body of the deceased, clothe the corpse, and then take it to
the cemetery for burial. The head of the family led whatever
prayers or psalms were recited. No historical record of a Roman
Church ritual for a funeral exists before the seventh century!
That recorded funeral ritual stated that the Eucharist be giv-
en to the dying, then after death the body be carried to church
where prayers are recited and the gospel of the death of Jesus
read. The deceased was then taken in procession to the cemetery. A universal church rite for Christian burial did not exist for
another two hundred years. Late in the ninth century, funerals
were conducted in various ways according to diverse customs
of different local Christian churches.

Another piece of the liturgical celebration of Christian death
is the wake or vigil service. There were various traditions, but
typically it was held the night before the funeral. Until about
the middle of the last century, recalling that funerals were originally family affairs, the wake was held in the family home of
the deceased. Today, convenience, along with other practical issues, has given rise to having the wake service in the funeral
home chapel. A visitation and wake can be, but traditionally
are not, the same thing. A visitation provides an opportunity
to pay one's respect by viewing the body of the deceased and
expressing sympathy to the family, but it is not a prayer service.
A wake or vigil service, however, combines viewing and praying privately at the casket of the deceased, an opportunity to
express condolences to the family, and a ritual prayer service
that includes biblical readings and prayers. Typically this vigil
service is led by the pastor or another church minister, lay or
ordained. Prior to the reforms of the Second Vatican Council,
the prayer service of the wake most often consisted only of the

communal praying of the rosary. Recently, because of crowded schedules, the wake and visitation service have sometimes been moved and condensed to an hour or so prior to the funeral service. Also, in some places, it is customary to have the wake and funeral services at night, and then the interment service the next morning as a private family affair.

Again, if after making every effort to receive a proper Christian burial it is denied, consider composing your own Exodus Christian funeral ritual. As you plan this funeral, remember that it can be as simple as a gathering at the funeral home, a burial service in the cemetery, or a memorial celebration at home after cremation or donation of the body. It can be a more formal funeral service with burial or cremation following. Or it can be composed of all three: the wake, the funeral or memorial service, and the burial ritual at the cemetery. Personnel at the funeral home or a local hospice should be able to help you find a non-denominational minister if you want one and also provide other guidance to help you plan a ritual celebration of this most significant of life's passages.

Prayer at the Death of an Exodus Christian

Any adult can lead this prayer; preferably it will be someone who knew the deceased. If the body of the deceased is present, invite everyone to gather nearby.

Prayer Leader:

We gather here in the presence of the Mystery of Death. Regardless of our age or health, the presence of death is inescapable in life. But here tonight (today) we are sitting close to death, which we fear. Yet if we believe in God, then death is but the Dark Angel who comes to carry us back again to God, from whom we have all come. By our presence here we express our

desire to share in the grief of _____'s family and closest friends.

In silence, let us now pray.

Allow a sufficient period of silence.

Come, Holy Spirit,
gather up the silent prayers of our hearts
and blend them together into a single prayer
of sorrow, hope, and promise.
Amen.

Suggested Readings:
Book of Wisdom 3:1–6, 9
Romans 6:3–4, 8–9
Matthew 11:25–30
John 6: 37–40

*The prayer leader may say a few words after the reading or invite oth-
ers to do so. Reflection on the reading, how it relates to the deceased,
and heartfelt memories of the deceased are all appropriate here.*

Communal Praying of Psalm 23
This might be done with several readers or with a communal
response like "The Lord is my shepherd" repeated between
each verse.

Prayer Leader:
We proclaim that our Lord, the Good Shepherd, has indeed guided _____ through the valley of death and dark-
ness, and has now set a feasting table for him/her in the house
of the Lord where he/she shall dwell forever. We profess our

belief in such a loving and providing God as we pray together the prayer that Jesus himself gave to us:

Pray together the Lord's Prayer

Prayer Leader:
In the Lord's Prayer we have asked for our daily bread, and now we ask God to give daily consolation to _____'s family and friends who are grieving his/her death.

> Gentle God,
> Bless these whom _____ loved in this life
> with the strength of your Holy Spirit.
> They now confront the empty, hollow spaces
> that his/her death has created in their lives and
>   hearts.
>
> Bless these who loved _____,
> after they have wept and properly mourned his
>   departure,
> strengthen them with your courage to again enter into
>   the flow of life.
> Bless each of us here now as we depart with your
>   grace.
> May we live mindful each day of our own death,
> and better able to love and live life fully.
> Amen.

Conclude with greeting each other with an embrace or kiss of peace, with laying flowers at the casket, or another gesture of farewell.

A Letter Regarding the Celebration of the Lord's Supper

Dear Anointed Companions in Christ,

As disciples of Christ Jesus, whom tradition has revered as a priest, prophet, and king, Christians are "the anointed ones." The night before his death, while at table, he gave an inheritance to his disciples of a memorial meal of his love and Spirit that we now call the Lord's Supper, Mass, or the Eucharist. The celebrating of this memorial meal has become connected with the rituals of marriage and funerals, and various other significant occasions in life. Today in Christian churches an ordained minister conducts this ritual of the Lord's Supper, but this was not a requirement in the early Christian church since they understood the words of Jesus, "Do this in memory of me," as being directed to all his disciples.

Since Jesus was not the creator of rituals, it is significant to ponder just what he intended. Ask yourself the question, "Do *what* in memory of me?" Historically, his Last Supper invitation has been understood in a limited, if not ritualistic, way to mean, "repeat these gestures and words over bread and wine." His invitation could also imply to give away yourself in love, service, and suffering to those you cherish and to all peoples. Understanding his dying request in this way makes it a way of life and the recipe for holiness. It is impossible to know the thinking of those earliest post-resurrection, pre-institutional church Christians. As they remembered while breaking bread and sharing the common cup, and experienced the mysterious presence of the risen Jesus, did they see that meal experience as a mystical reminder of how they, who were to follow him, were supposed to live? And should not you who have been baptized into Christ make that mystical remembrance a daily ritual of dedication for yourself?

To stand before a crowd or a group of people in a church ritual and recite Jesus' words of investing himself over bread and wine can be a real power rush. To humbly empty yourself, pouring out your time, your attention and love, your very flesh and blood in an ongoing give-away to others is a subservient, sacred way to "do this in memory of me."

This ancient ritual evokes a desire to partake, even among those who no longer go to church. This being the case, what options do they have? For over two millennia the memorial meal of Jesus has taken various forms, beginning with a simple table ritual of a small group to an elaborate high church ritual accompanied by the majestic organ music of Bach. The Gospel of Luke gives us another expression in what could be called "The Emmaus Eucharist." It recounts how two disciples—hope-deprived by the death of the man they thought would be the Messiah—encounter a stranger while traveling on the road to Emmaus. They invite him to share supper with them as they approach the village. In the breaking of the bread, they recognize the stranger as the risen Christ, then he vanishes from their sight. In that first recorded remembrance of the Lord's Supper, the hearts of the two disciples were set ablaze by experiencing the presence of the Christ in the breaking of the bread.

If as a non-ordained Christian you long to experience the risen Christ in a remembrance meal like the Last Supper, consider celebrating an Emmaus meal. The two disciples in Luke's account were not ordained, so follow their example. The rubrics of such an Emmaus meal are extremely simple: some bread and wine, two or more believers, and the reading of an abridged account from Luke's Gospel (Lk 24:30–31). You might also include

the words of Jesus over the bread and wine at the Last Supper
(Lk 22: 14–20). And by all means follow the remembrance with
an actual festive meal together.

Another ritual expression of a remembrance meal from
the pre-institutional church comes to us by way of Saint Paul.
Around the year 57, twenty-seven or so years after Jesus' death,
Paul wrote in 1 Corinthians 11: 23–26:

> On the night he was handed over, he took
> bread, and after he had given thanks, broke it
> and said, 'This is my body that is for you. Do
> this in remembrance of me.' In the same way
> he took the cup saying, 'This cup is the new
> covenant of my blood. Do this, as often as you
> drink it, in remembrance of me.'

Note the beautiful briefness and ambiguity of this early ritual. Paul believed that Christ was truly present in the bread
and in the body of gathered believers. The New Testament
gives examples of how the disciples came together weekly in
private homes to celebrate a sacred remembrance meal that
was customarily led by either the host or hostess of the home
where they had gathered. This event occurred at a friendship
meal that included the recounting of the Lord's Supper meal
(as it became known) prior to the common sharing of the actual meal. Scholars believe the separation of the actual meal
from the Lord's Supper was gradual, but by around 150 to 200
these fellowship meals were celebrated only on special occasions. With the gradual evolution of the Lord's Supper into a
ritual meal that included parts of the Jewish Sabbath morning
service of readings, the elders or clergy became the customary
celebrants. This brief historical review only reinforces the central place in the lives of Christians that the Lord's Supper has

consistently occupied, and also the gradual evolution of clergy or elders as the only ones who could rightfully preside at these celebrations.

As you personally consider activating your baptismal and apostolic prerogative of remembering the Lord's Supper, I would like to add a few words about the readings of scripture that are now commonplace in Christian celebrations of the Lord's Supper. Recently, a friend spoke to me frankly about the scripture readings at Sunday worship, saying he found they lacked coherence with actual life. He complained that the readings he heard at worship were all from ancient ages, and so did not help him live in the present world or to imagine the future. He lamented that priests educated in scripture and religious history knew the meaning of those texts, but ordinary people didn't, and asked why even include them since no one understands or remembers them once they have left church.

I agree with him. As a people who are constantly bombarded by media, with people talking to us 24/7, we have learned not to listen. While the scripture readings at the celebration of the Eucharist are beautiful and link us to the ancient past, sadly they often fall on deaf ears.

We cannot expect the institutional church to drop the ancient tradition of scripture readings in church rituals, even if they are not understood or grasped by many, if not most, of the faithful. This tradition began in the early, mostly Jewish church that adapted the format of the synagogue service with its several readings, and placed it at the beginning of the memory meal of the Last Supper. However, are biblical readings, especially if their content isn't understood or doesn't relate to contemporary life, necessary for home church worship?

For a home church celebration of the Lord's Supper, instead of these readings consider perhaps only one or two sentences from the scriptures followed by a period of silent recollection. Instead of reading a gospel passage, consider retelling the gospel, including the words of Jesus for the breaking of the bread and passing the wine at his final supper. This non-reading, but rather telling, would be a return to the apostolic age when this was part of the oral tradition of the church. The sharing of bread and wine (or grape juice for those who prefer) could be followed by a period of silent reflection; then perhaps a brief spoken reflection by someone present on how you can integrate the meaning of this holy meal into daily life.

Prayer for an Emmaus Meal

The host or hostess of the meal can serve as prayer leader or invite another person to do so. After all have gathered at table, the leader begins:

Come; let us be united in peace and in love as we gather to celebrate this holy meal and remember the Lord's Supper. With reverence we acknowledge here in our midst the promised presence of the risen Christ. Blessed is this home church, the dwelling place of the Holy since Christ is present in expressions of love and kindness, in acts of service, and in the generous forgiving and pardoning of faults. Aware of how we have come here from busy lives and from a world of turmoil, we pause now in silence to be conscious that we are gathered in the presence of Christ whose love has brought us together.

Pause for silent recollection.

We remember our communion with all who are present and with whom we are about to share this holy meal (short pause), as well as our communion with all the Church, the Body of Christ, with whom we are united in spirit if not in body *(short pause).*

Having entered into this holy communion of faith we are now ready to celebrate the this holy meal with Christ as our host, he whose fondest prayer was that we be united as one flock and with one shepherd to lead us.

Read or tell from memory a brief scripture passage such as those mentioned in the above letter. Then the prayer leader or another person speaks briefly about how the celebration of this meal of remembrance connects to daily gospel living.

After a period for silent recollection, invite each person to mention for what they give thanks this day and for what needs they would like the group to pray.

After all have spoken, the leader continues:

>Good and gracious God,
>We ask your blessings on this bread and this cup.
>May they be for us holy nourishment.
>May we, like the disciples on the road to Emmaus,
>recognize you as we share their life-sustaining
>   goodness.

Bread and cup are passed and shared.

>Gathered and united here at this holy table,
>make us one with all Christians and their leaders,
>with all those who worship you in synagogues,
>   mosques, shrines, and temples;
>one indeed with all believers and all unbelievers—
>all of whom are precious to you as your children.

By this our prayer of unity and communion,
move us closer to realizing the vision of Jesus, your son,
of one flock and one shepherd who is you.
Unite us with all the holy dead,
especially those of our families whom we now
    remember in silence.

Pause for silent remembrance.

With faith we acknowledge their unseen presence at
    this table
together with the risen Christ and Mary, the Mother of
    Jesus,
with the apostles and all the saints.
In union with them we praise you through your son,
    Jesus Christ.

Let us open the windows of our hearts and souls
to receive the flood of blessings God desires to give us.
May the Wind of the Spirit flow through the open
    windows of our hearts,
filling us with inspiration to live prophetically,
and by our lives and deeds may we broadcast to all
the good news of Christ, risen and among us.

As the Priestly People of God,
from the fullness we have received
through the open windows of our hearts,
let us send forth the blessings of peace from this holy
    meal
to all peoples, to all life on the earth, and out into the
    universe.
Let us celebrate this meal together in service, peace
    and joy.

We pray in the name of Jesus, our Lord and Savior. Amen.

A festive communal meal follows.

FIVE

The Apostolic
Exodus Letters

Letter to Timothy and All Priests and Pastors Encouraging Compassion Toward Exodus Christians

Dear Tim, Brothers in the Clergy, and Fellow Sinners,

I write to you as contemporary apostles, fellow evangelists, and brother pastors who are sent to forth to proclaim the Good News. Being retired, I have the advantage of viewing today's problems in the Church from a different vantage and so exhort you to be good shepherds, as was Jesus of Galilee, your model and example. I realize you yourselves have not become part of the ongoing exodus from the Church. While you have continued to give pastoral care to the faithful who attend church, you also are pastors to today's Exodus Christians.

I'm responding to your letter, in which you spoke fondly of former times in the Church, "when the number one issue was how to empower the laity and engage them more fully in the life of church, and how the Church has now sadly recycled itself back to former days." Indeed, today's church agenda seems bent on the restoration of clerical power instead of empowering the laity. Both you and I are able to remember those heady days when the issues that defined the Church as a compassionate institution were the struggle for social justice, racial and sexual equality, peace, and just wages for workers.

I agree with your observation that the Church "will cycle back one of these days." However, I don't see that return happening anytime in the near future! Even the best expectation for such a graced movement would take thirty to fifty years, and by that time you will have reached the age of retirement—or may have died! Judging from the strong entrenchment of conservatives in church leadership today, it isn't unrealistic to think of a fifty- to hundred-year timetable for any major changes in the church! Meanwhile, accepting that historical ecclesial possibility, what do you and other pastors do to apostolically minister to the faithful? There are a couple of options once you silently grit your teeth and stoically accept the present situation, feeling impotent to change it. This first option is a form of "early retirement," where pastors restrict themselves to executing the rules of church authorities while struggling to maintain their parish programs and ministering to those who continue to attend church. Anything other than this seems impossible if one considers the workload placed on overworked pastors that leaves them with little if any time to imagine or creatively fashion alternatives for religious renewal.

A second option is to expand your concept of pastoral ministry beyond those who faithfully attend Sunday worship. As a pastor, you have been called to imitate Jesus, the Good Shepherd, and that pastoral discipleship implies compassionate care of those who no longer choose to be inside the fold of your parish. Returning to your role model of Jesus, recall when a foreigner, a Canaanite woman, petitioned Jesus for help, and he dismissed her, replying, "My mission is to the lost sheep of Israel!" His reply, I feel, is most significant for you and worthy of your reflection, since it unveils a most interesting question. "Were his first Jewish disciples—Peter, John, Andrew, and the others—lost sheep?" Other than the publican tax collector, Matthew (whose profession made him unclean and therefore a religious outsider), the gospels don't indicate that the other disciples were lost, that is, fallen-away Jews who didn't observe all the many laws of the orthodox and perhaps didn't attend communal worship on a regular basis. Yet Jesus said quite plainly that his mission was to the lost sheep of Israel and appears to have befriended these lost ones and may have made them members of his inner circle of disciples. Eating and associating with, and spiritually caring for the needs of those living outside of orthodoxy Judaism were some of the accusations leveled against Jesus by the orthodox religious leaders of his day.

As a pastor, you realize that in addition to those who have exited the Church, there are those who attend weekly worship yet feel lost, religiously homeless, and spiritually dispossessed. With earnest prayer, keenly attune your pastoral radar and strive to be attentive to the silent suffering of those among the faithful who seek nourishment. Prayerfully sandpaper your sensitivity so as to be able to compassionately care for their needs and those of the majority of your fold who happen to no longer come to church. They are the spiritually homeless who, after serious spiritual searching, have become part of the majority of believers that could be called Exodus Christians.

None of us enjoy hearing negative reports about our work or the institutions we represent. Few pastors have the courage to invite their parishioners to critique the liturgies they lead, their homilies, or the actions taken by their local or global church. Be not fooled by the crowds who attend your services in this age when seven out of ten Christians no longer come to church on a regular basis. Instead, seriously ask those who no longer come to church why they have stopped.

Pray that the Spirit of Bravery inspires you to ask those kinds of difficult questions that are necessary to explore the reasons for the departure of so many of the faithful. Pray especially to the Spirit not for the gift of tongues but of ears: the gift of open, nonjudgmental ears, so you might truly listen to the answers you hear and then, as far as it is possible, correct whatever is necessary. This pastoral correction is, of course, critical today, since the number of those departing will increase yearly. Jesus tells the parable of a compassionate shepherd who left the ninety-nine faithful sheep to go and search for the single lost one. Today the number of lost sheep is not one out of a hundred, but closer to sixty-six out of a hundred, and their number grows larger daily.

How are you to view the majority of baptized Catholic Christians who no longer attend church weekly? Are they not like those thousands of men and women who followed Jesus out to a deserted place where he had gone with his disciples to find some peace and quiet? When Jesus looked upon that vast crowd, the author of Mark's Gospel tells us "his heart was moved to pity for them, for they were like sheep without a shepherd; and he began to teach them many things" (Mk 6: 34). Like the hundreds of thousands today, they were also without a sheepfold or a shepherd pastor, and we are told that before Jesus fed them with bread and fish, he taught them. No record is given in the gospels as to what he taught these lost sheep, but whatever it was, we can be sure that it nourished them more than did the bread!

I propose that Jesus taught that hungry crowd by prophetic deed and word the same things he taught throughout his entire ministry. Over and over, the gospels tell us that he reached out to care for those who didn't keep the kosher rules of diet, conduct, and worship, and those who sinned. To these he taught that love was the fulfillment of all the countless ritual laws and even the commandments. In loving their neighbor by generous deeds of compassion and sharing with the needy, by loving their enemies, they were expressing fidelity to the ancient religion of their birth. The author of Mark's Gospel had no need to detail Jesus' teaching at the multiplication of the bread and fish, since his entire living gospel was saturated with the same message.

I conclude, Timothy, with the prayer that the same Spirit with whom you were gifted at your ordination will inspire you to be a compassionate pastor-shepherd who will lovingly care for all those today who no longer regularly go to church. By your love of them—your efforts to tend to their spiritual needs—you will witness to them the all-accepting love of God and the touch of the living presence of the Risen Good Shepherd.

Second Letter to Pastor Timothy About How a Pastoral Attitude of Compassion Leads to Sainthood and Christhood

Dear Tim,

I received your thoughtful response to my letter and empathize with the tension of your struggle. It is not easy to be a faithful disciple of Christ, striving to live his gospel teachings while also being a loyal minister of your church, obedient to her many regulations. The Master calls you to wrestle with this vocational struggle between discipleship and being an ordained minister of the Church. Christ also calls you and your brother pastors to be kindhearted and caring. To be a compassionate pastor-shepherd requires seeing others with the eyes of Jesus. With the gift of those eyes you will be able to look with loving empathy upon today's hungry shepherd-less Christians. They may not be registered in your parish, nor do they financially contribute to it, and as a result it is easy to dismiss them when they appear at your door asking to have their children baptized, their marriages witnessed, or their beloved dead buried.

Your time as a typical busy pastor is already consumed caring for those who faithfully come to church every week and contribute to your parish. To minister to the spiritual needs of those who are, practically speaking, no longer your parishioners, who lack a sheepfold, requires the extra-large heart of a saint and a prophet—a gentle heart like that of the Master. When you are asked to perform pastoral care for these, the religiously homeless ones, you will find yourself, as did old Jacob, wrestling with God. The easy way out of a spiritual tussle is to place Church above God since your institutional Church has definite rules and policies defining just who may and may not receive the sacraments. Do not fear to follow the guidance of the Spirit of God, who always calls each of us, regardless of the cost, to be loyal to the greater law of love. Versed in theology, you know that the voice of your conscience is always the final judge of how best to interpret the laws of the Church.

If your conscience makes it impossible for you to perform a marriage (or whatever sacrament or service), be a pastor. Invite whoever has come to your door or is on the phone to engage with you in a pastoral visit. Usually, you will find that their real need is to be married in a church or in a religious service, since they want God to bless their union. You can discuss with them the option of having a minister of another church perform the religious service. Or you can suggest they have a civil ceremony followed by a celebration of family and friends before whom they prayerfully exchange vows of marriage. As a pastor, you can be of great assistance by suggesting various rituals, prayers, and scriptural readings for such a domestic church home ritual. Whenever you respond in such a Christ-like way, they will experience in you God's unconditional love and that of the Risen Jesus, who promised to always be with his people.

A good pastor-shepherd is also a prophet, one who proclaims the will and mind of God. Jesus of Nazareth was just such a prophet, who by his loving and gracious actions and words made known the mind and heart of God. The God of Jesus desired the salvation and pastoral care of all peoples, not simply of those who were outwardly religious and obedient to religious laws. Every true prophet knows that to be called to give living witness to the mind and heart of God isn't easy and is usually costly. Be prepared for serious consequences if you choose to respond in a prophetic pastoral way toward the shepherd-less at your door.

As a pastor, be mindful that the lost and homeless sheep will be apprehensive about ever coming to your front door except when in dire need of the sacraments. Instead, you might encounter them anywhere, since they are everywhere. When you do encounter them in the supermarket, at a ballgame, or after weddings and funerals, consider that encounter a graced event. It is like the graced opportunity the Good Samaritan found lying in the ditch on the road to Jericho, an opportunity to which he responded with empathy, grace, and generosity. Do not, as did the priest in that parable, pass by, haughtily ignoring one in need. Regardless of the place or time when these Exodus Christians approach, you will be short of time! That seems to be the one constant. So steal, make, or invent time, and if this is not possible, then try to arrange for another time when that person can visit with you about his or her pastoral needs. Be guided by the pastoral example of the Master, whose most significant exchanges with the religious homeless of his day took place at dinners, water wells, or traveling on the road. From the gospels it is clear that he always found or created the time necessary to minister to their needs.

The contemporary departure of a majority of believers from attending church is a reality—an unpleasant, controversial, yet sacred reality. It should raise critical self-examinations of our liturgical worship, our preaching, and the communal-family nature of our congregation in order to understand the reasons why people are not attending church. Or can the source of this major contemporary exodus out of the Church be God? Is it not possible that what is happening now is the work of God who once again is, as Isaiah said, "doing something new"? If this is the case, then as one ordained by and for the People of God, choose not to be a priestly passive bystander to this "something new" but rather a midwife to its birth. Only clerical blindness or fear of facing distasteful realities can blame this modern exodus on laziness, indifference, or relativism. Clearly, the Spirit's finger is prodding us to wrestle with this major migration out of the Church. We are challenged to prayerfully question what its source and meaning are, even if the institutional Church prefers to condemn instead of asking the hard questions.

Finally, I strongly encourage you to both support and find support among your brother pastors who are of the same mind as you. The source of the dynamic energy of the early church was that it was composed of small groups of believers. So be in communion and communication by e-mail or by small group gatherings with these clergy friends. Encourage and challenge one another to be prophetic not by words but by example. And whenever you gather in small groups for these ongoing sacraments of confirmation and inspiration, be aware of the powerful, invisible presence of the Teacher and Pastor-Shepherd who promised where two or three of his disciples were gathered in his name, he would be present there among them.

As I conclude this letter, I am aware that I have used the word "compassionate" perhaps too frequently in this letter. But of all the virtues needed by today's clergy, surely it ranks in first place as an expression of merciful love. So Timothy, peace and fortitude to you, and most of all may you be daily drenched in the prophetic Spirit of Compassion.

SIX

A closing Letter

To Exodus Christians of Today and Beyond

Dear Twenty-first Century Christians,

In this closing letter, I want to share with you the prophetic words of that great twentieth century theologian, Karl Rahner: "If there are any Christians in the twenty-first century, they will be mystics!"

Rahner's prediction seems to be coming true today and is central to understanding the New Exodus. Christians go to church seeking an experience of the sacred, and when they fail to find it, they simply leave to seek God elsewhere. Dismiss any idea that it is impossible for you to be a mystic! Reject the idea that such an experience is limited only to the super-saints. Has not everyone at some time in their life had a mystical experience, where they've been taken out of themselves by a sexual ecstasy, a powerful piece of music, a work of visual art, or a deeply moving religious experience? To be totally absorbed to the extent that you forget yourself by being caught up in some wondrous experience of nature, like the birth of a child, or by being inspired is to have undergone a mystical experience.

Any who claim to be non-mystics would have to be those living exclusively on the veneer of life. Perhaps somehow in childhood their souls were severely crippled so that they are now immune to wonder—to the wonderful awesomeness of life. Imbedded in our DNA is a yearning for the mystical or supernatural. It is to satisfy this hunger that people seek religion, since it alone claims to offer the supernatural.

Jesus promised, "Where two or three of you are gathered in my name, I will be there in your midst." That promised mystical presence isn't a bodily presence, nor is it automatic. We have all been in Christian groups of two or more where Jesus definitely was not present! For the risen Christ to be present we must come together not simply as fellow believers or members of the same church, but in his name. It isn't sufficient to simply use his literal name, "Jesus of Nazareth" or "Jesus Christ," or any of his other names, but rather to gather in what is contained in his name. The ancients believed a person somehow became present in the pronouncing of his or her name. The person of Jesus was love incarnate, he was God's love made flesh, so to come together "in his name" is to gather in love, peace, and acceptance.

In your underground gatherings, guard carefully against the presence of the dark forces of anger, prejudice, and pride! Your small catacomb churches will surely attract disgruntled Christians who are angry at the Church, the clergy, or the hierarchy. If you wish your worship to be mystical by having the true presence of Christ, then be prepared to deal with those whose anger at the institutional Church, while understandable, is contagiously toxic. Guard your small gatherings also from the prejudiced feelings of being elite, the select few, or in any way being superior to those who still faithfully attend church. One final word of caution: Remember one of the principles of liberation theology, "The oppressed take on the ways of their oppressors!" Be prepared for the likelihood that among your members there will be those who were oppressed by the rigidity of the institutional Church. In or out of positions of authority, they may become as domineering and inflexible as were the leaders of the church they have now left behind.

The Church of Tomorrow

You are the future of Christianity! As I write you I wonder, by mid-century when your children or grandchildren will become the majority of the believers, what will weekly worship be like in America? Is religion in America recycling itself back to what it was like in 1776 when only about one out of six persons belonged to a church? If this does prove true, when attending any gathering of fifty-some persons, only eight of them would be members of a church. Thomas Jefferson said that every generation was a new republic, and surely the same is true for religion; each generation is a new church. Just as your expression of religion is different than that of your parents, so your children's will be of yours. If they are Christians, the same basic Christian truths will be present, yet they will be expressed and ritualized differently than they are today. This has been clearly the case century after century since the days when Jesus lived and proclaimed the Gospel, even if some religious leaders are prone to claim that nothing has changed. It is only natural to be concerned about the shape and expression of the faith for the generations that will follow this Exodus generation. It is natural to desire that your children's children practice the faith and be able to benefit from it as you have.

Your influence on the future of Christianity, however, will depend upon the Spirit of God, and your willingness to be mystical martyr-witnesses who follow your consciences as best you can with the help of God. With hope and prayer we must all plant the seeds of truth as announced in the Gospel and in the practice of ancient Christianity. Then we leave the harvest of the future to God. In closing, let us not forget that, along with those of the institutional church, those of the underground catacomb church of this century are the future of Christianity. Since this is your destiny, set for yourselves personal goals to become holy, prayerful, and ever-ready in all circumstances to be priestly martyr-witnesses of Christ.

Yours in joyful hope,

NOTES

for your own journey

Edward Hays is the co-founder and a moving spirit of Forest of Peace Publishing. He is the author of over thirty best-selling books on contemporary spirituality. Many bear his own art. He has also served as director of Shantivanam, a Midwest center for contemplative prayer, and as a chaplain of the state penitentiary in Lansing, Kansas. He has spent extended periods of pilgrimage in the Near East, the Holy Land, and India. He continues his ministry as a prolific writer and painter.

More from Edward Hays

Chasing Joy
Musings on Life in a Bittersweet World

Forty reflections filled with hints and exercises for cultivating a deeply rooted spirit of joy in spite of living in a not-so-joyful world.

"Edward Hays's mystical sensibility and unbridled imagination makes his vision of Christianity consistently fresh and invigorating."
Frederic and Mary Ann Brussat
SpiritualityandPractice.com

ISBN: 9780939516780 / 192 pages / $12.95

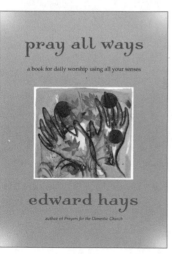

Pray All Ways
A Book for Daily Worship Using All Your Senses

Edward Hays's pioneering book on prayer offers a unique interpretation of the biblical command to "pray always" as a call to pray creatively, at all times, and in every circumstance. Learn how to pray with your eyes and nose, your taste buds and hunger pains, and your hands and feet.

"There are few people who consistently give us both depth and breadth—while never closing that clever and humorous edge—as Ed Hays."
Richard Rohr, O.F.M.
Center for Action and Contemplation

ISBN: 9780939516810 / 160 pages / $12.95

Forest of Peace
from Ave Maria Press, Inc.
Notre Dame, IN
www.forestofpeace.com

A Ministry of the Indiana Province of Holy Cross

Keycode: FD9Ø6Ø8ØØØØ